THE 30-MINUTE VEGETARIAN COOKBOOK

COOKING HEALTHY, DELICIOUS VEGETARIAN RECIPES IN 30 MINUTES. EVERYONE WILL LOVE YOUR DISHES.

TABLE OF CONTENTS

Chapter 3: Salads and dressings   48

4

Chapter 4: Lunch 90

Chapter 5: Dinner 109

Chapter 6: Snacks and Desserts 169

Conclusion   187

Introduction

Vegetarianism refers to a lifestyle that excludes the consumption of all forms of meat including pork, chicken, beef, lamb, venison, fish, and shells. Depending on a person belief and lifestyle, vegetarianism has different spectrums. There are vegetarians, who like to consume products that come from animals such as milk, eggs, cream and cheese. On the other end of that spectrum are the vegans. Vegans never consume meat or any product that comes from animals.

I firmly believe every decision we make in life, regardless of how well-calculated the move is, has good and bad consequences. Your dietary habit is no exception; in fact, your food choices significantly impact overall health and wellbeing. Precisely, when it comes to dieting, the rule of thumb here is simple; proper nutrition results in healthy living and satisfaction.

However, we live in a world where new dietary habits crop up every day. Besides, today, people are redefining the old dietary practices to suit the modern lifestyle. New dietary habits, coupled with the complexity of today's lifestyle, put the world on a collision course with the principles of healthy living. What encourages me, however, is the fact that some dietary practices like vegetarianism have stood the test of time.

However, if you have decided to go vegetarian life, congratulations, you have made a brilliant decision. This because commitment to vegetarianism is a dedication to good health. And luckily for you, I have written this book to hold your hand during the transition. The book will see you through the journey, opening up horizons of whole new meals that you will adore.

Regardless of your reason for going vegetarian, you will adore this cookbook. Whether it is for religious or health purposes, I have unpacked the information you need and served it up in a way that is easy to understand. Besides, I will give you cooking tips that will help you nail vegetarianism and make it part of your lifestyle. Trust me, the journey will be bumpy, but with this cookbook, you have a partner to keep you going even when things seem to be grinding to a halt.

As if that is not enough, this book has simple recipes to get you started. Everything from salads, appetizers, and mains, each Directions is designed to complement your health and those crazy cravings. I went for recipes with five ingredients or less, to give you a smooth ride in the kitchen.

Trust me, with this cookbook; you will love vegetables even before you know it. This cookbook is not only the best vegetarian book with tons of recipes but also a simple guide to vegetarianism and benefits to it. If looking forward to vegetarianism for the rest of your life, this cookbook is for you.

Chapter 1: Introduction to vegetarian.

Vegetarian diets are most often much lower in sugars and fat than a meat based diet; though just cutting meat out is no guarantee of weight loss. Vegetarians are still tempted by junk food, highly processed foods and other unhealthy foods too. If you are planning on losing weight by becoming a vegetarian then you need to follow some other basic weight loss strategies to ensure you lose the weight you want.

One of the main benefits to you of the vegetarian diet is that it is lower in saturated fat (though be wary of convenience vegetarian foods which are high in these unhealthy fats) and has a higher intake of fresh fruit and vegetables. This makes a vegetarian leaner than a meat eater, so long as they are not a junk food addict.

Being a vegan means even less saturated fat as you do not eat dairy or eggs, so technically you can lose more weight. However, it is down to your personal preference, your lifestyle and your tastes. Going vegan for a few weeks can help kick start your weight loss.

Just stopping eating meat isn't going to help you lose weight if you are still consuming huge amounts of calories every day. You will need to discipline yourself and control your calorie intake like you would on any diet. However, remember that vegetables in particular are low in calories and most diets instruct you to "pile 'em high" on your plate!

Just watch your portion sizes, particularly with the more fattening foods that you eat; the same goes for restaurants. Prepare your meals in advance and plan what you are going to eat and you will find it much easier to lose weight. Also make sure you have some healthy, low fat snacks around so you are less likely to reach for a candy bar.

Try to avoid frying food when you can and bake, steam or grill instead because it is lower in fat and much healthier for you.

In order to lose weight reliably you will need to increase your exercise levels to burn fat and excess calories. Regular cardio and weight training will help to improve your health and help you process food better. You can lose some weight as a vegetarian but to really turbo-charge your weight loss you need to incorporate exercise into your daily regime. Join a gym, get a personal trainer and start working out because you will find your weight loss speeds up and that you lose inches as you start to firm up your muscles.

The main component of your diet will be vegetables and fruits, together with beans and whole grains. With all meats and fish eliminated from your diet you are already eating many of the foods that are recommended by diet plans to help you lose weight. Studies have shown that a low fat vegan diet alone will help you to lose 1lb a week without including exercise or any other factors!

Be aware though that if you are loading up on pasta, cereal and breads (high carbohydrate / low nutrition) then you will struggle to lose weight. Eating too many sugary foods or the meat substitutes is also going to contribute to you not losing weight. Remember that by applying these principles to your vegetarian diet you will speed up your weight loss and improve your health further.

A vegan will eliminate all meat products from their diet including eggs, dairy and gelatine. Typically a vegan will avoid any products that are made from animals such as leather, wool, down, silk and so on. Many vegans choose to follow this lifestyle because they have care deeply for animals and the environment.

Vegetarians however will wear leather, wool and silk and many will eat eggs and dairy products. Most vegetarians will avoid products that contain gelatine though some will quietly ignore it as it is in such a tiny quantity. It is your choice which you follow at the end of the day.

Nutritionally there is not a huge amount of difference between a pure vegetarian and a vegan; the latter will need a vitamin B12 supplement. A lacto-ovo vegetarian should not need this supplement as they will get it from eggs and dairy. For those that choose the vegan approach it is usually related to their love and respect for animals. From a weight loss point of view, a vegan diet can help to kick-start your weight loss and help you lose an extra couple of pounds when you need it.

Whether you start off as a vegetarian and do weeks of vegan eating or what type of vegetarian diet you choose to follow is entirely up to you. Make sure you have thought through all the different options and selected the right type of diet for you.

Whilst the vegetarian diet is going to help you to lose weight, it is also going to help to improve your health. A lot of research has been performed in to the benefits of vegetarianism, and the result is the federal government even recommend that the majority of your daily calories come from vegetables, fruits and grain products.

It is estimated that around 70% of all diseases, including a third of all cancers are caused by diet! Vegetarians have a lower risk of obesity, high blood pressure, diabetes, coronary artery disease and cancers including prostate, stomach, breast, oesophageal and colon cancer. You can already see the benefits of cutting out meat!

You will be interested in knowing that vegetarians are typically healthier than the average American, particularly when it comes to reversing heart disease and reducing the risks of cancers. A low fat vegetarian diet has been proven to be the best way to stop coronary artery disease progressing or to prevent it.

Every year, over a million people in American die from cardiovascular disease; it's the number one killer in the USA. However, the mortality rate from this disease is significantly lower in vegetarians due to the lower cholesterol levels and that you consume less saturated fat. A vegetarian will consume more anti-oxidants, more fiber and more vitamins and minerals.

The standard Western diet is high in processed foods full of chemicals, sugar and salt and low in plant based foods. This diet is actually killing us all slower. The obesity statistics are shocking and the associated health problems even worse.

Between the years of 1986 and 1992 the Preventive Medicine Research Institute in Sausalito California conducted a study in to the vegetarian diet. They discovered that an overweight person who ate a low fat vegetarian diet lost, on average, twenty four pounds in year one and in five year's time had still kept the weight off. This weight was lost without feeling hungry, measuring portions or counting calories.

Studies have also shown that a vegetarian diet will extend your life by around thirteen years of good health! Meat eaters will typically not only have a shorter lifespan but will also suffer from more disabilities at the end of their lives. Studies have also shown that meat eaters also experience sexual and cognitive dysfunction at a younger age.

A fringe benefit of vegetarianism is that your risk of food borne illness is dramatically reduced. According to CDC statistics there are 76,000,000 food borne illnesses each year across the United States. The majority of these illnesses come from meat and seafood!

The vegetarian diet also eases the symptoms of the menopause, particularly as soy is the best natural source of phytoestrogens, but they are also found in many other vegetables too. As women often gain weight during the menopause as their metabolism slows down, a low fat vegetarian diet can help keep the extra pounds off.

Another advantage of the vegetarian diet is that your energy levels increase. As you are not spending so much of your energy digesting heavy foods. The foods you eat as a vegetarian tend to be more nutritious, meaning your body has the vitamins it needs to be healthy.

A good, balanced vegetarian diet is free from the saturated fats that clog up your arteries and restricts the oxygen supply to your body. Your diet will also be high in complex carbohydrates which give you more energy that lasts longer.

Vegetarians also help the environment with meat production causing deforestation, global warming and more. According to the EPA in the USA, animal and chemical waste runoff from factory farming causes over 173,000 miles of polluted streams and rivers.

Many of the toxins a human eats come from meat and seafood, with fish in particular storing heaving metals and carcinogens that cannot be removed. Many meat and dairy products also have high levels of growth hormones, steroids and antibiotics which are taken in to your body.

Around 70% of the grain produced in the USA is fed to animals. There are around seven billion livestock animals in the United States which consume five times more grain than the American population itself. The grain fed to animals is worth about $80 billion on the export market and would feed around 800 million people!

Every year over ten billion animals are slaughtered for human consumption, which is a major factor for many vegetarians in giving up meat. That and the treatment of animals – factory farming, force feeding, poor conditions and so on. What you may not realize is that state laws on animal cruelty specifically exclude farm animals from even the most basic, humane protection.

Being a vegetarian is cheaper, particular if you don't rely on the expensive textured vegetable protein used as a meat substitute. Around 10% of the average American's income is spent on meat. By cutting out the meat, on average, you could save around $4,000 a year!

The vegetarian's dinner plate is always full of color, which means they are full of vital vitamins and minerals. Yellow and orange foods are high in carotenoids, as are leafy green vegetables, which are also high in chlorophyll. Red and purple foods are high in anthocyanins. These are both important for your health and will help boost your immune system.

With so many personal and environmental benefits to being a vegetarian your plan to lose weight suddenly seems even more appealing. You will notice that as you lose weight you feel healthier, have more energy and are able to enjoy life more because of it.

Benefits of a Vegetarian Diet

Lower risk of stroke and obesity
Vegetarians contribute to be much more having knowledge of their food choices and generally never overeat or choose foods that are based on emotions, two practices that contribute significantly to obesity. The Paediatric Department at the University Hospital of Ghent in Belgium believes that a vegan diet is an excellent way to minimize the risk of stroke or obesity.

Get healthy skin
If you want to have healthy skin, you need to take the right amount of vitamins and minerals with plenty of water. The fruits and vegetables we eat are very rich in vitamins, minerals, and antioxidants. Because they are water-based, they can improve your intake of healthy nutrients when consumed raw. Many vegetarian foods are also rich in antioxidants that allow you to stay disease-free and have more youthful skin.

Reduce depression
According to studies, a vegetarian could be happier than his non-vegetarian counterparts. It was also found that a vegetarian had lower levels of depression and swinging mood profiles compared to the non-vegetarians. Besides,

most vegetarian diets contain an element of freshness, especially for organic products, therefore obligated to cleanse our mind and also keep our thoughts positive.

Reduce the risk of cataracts
According to a study by the Oxford University Nuffield Clinical Medicine Department, there is a close correlation between the risk of developing cataracts and our diet, higher risk for non-vegetarians or meat consumers, and a lower risk of being vegan.

Economical
Lastly, you will save a lot of money if you are vegetarian. Without a doubt, non-vegetarian foods are expensive compared to vegetarian foods.

Extend the life
Although many factors are due to an increase in life, it is possible to eat a vegetarian diet. The more fruits or vegetables you eat, the fewer toxins and chemicals you accumulate in your body, leading to healthier years and longer life.

Foods To *Eat* And Foods To Avoid

As a vegetarian you will avoid all meat and seafood products, though some will eat eggs and dairy. On top of this there are a lot of other things that a vegetarian can eat and this section is designed to help you understand how the vegetarian diet works and what foods you can eat and enjoy.

Grains

Grains are an important part of the vegetarian diet and it is recommended that you eat between five and seven servings per day, of which half should be whole grains. Grains include oats, barley, wheat, rice, bread and pasta, many of which are now fortified with vitamins such as zinc, iron and vitamin B-12 which are more commonly found in meat and seafood.

Proteins

Non-vegetarians get their protein from meat, but you will need to get your protein from other sources including beans, legumes, soy and nuts. For those who eat it, dairy and eggs are a good source of protein too. Iron normally comes from meat but instead you can find it in dry beans, lentils, soybeans, tofu, peas and spinach. Remember to consume foods rich in vitamin C at the same time as they help you absorb iron.

Fruits And Vegetables

Fruits and vegetables are consumed in large amounts by a vegetarian. Whether these are fresh or frozen is entirely up to you, but whichever you choose they are high in vitamins and minerals. You want between six and eight servings of vegetables every day and three or four of fruit. If you are not eating eggs or dairy then make sure you eat plenty of dark green leafy vegetables as they are high in nutrients your body needs.

Fats

We are taught that low fat diets are good for us, but your diet needs to be low in saturated fats. The proper fats are important for the operation of your body and you need around two servings per day. You need fats that are high in Omega-3 fatty acids which you can get from an ounce of nuts or seeds, a teaspoon of olive oil or two tablespoons of nut butter.

As a vegetarian you will be eating plenty of nutrient dense foods though because of the lack of meat, particularly if you are avoiding dairy and eggs, you may need to take some supplements to ensure you are getting the right nutrients.

Foods To Be Careful Of

As a vegetarian you will need to be careful about some of the foods you are eating because meat does creep into rather a lot of foods. This section will help you understand what foods you need to watch out for.

Soups are delicious and great for a vegetarian, but be careful when dining out or buying cans of soup as often they will be made with a chicken, beef or fish base. Make sure you ask in a restaurant and read the ingredients on the can just to be sure, but it is easy to make your own delicious soups at home!

A lot of salad dressings in restaurants are built on bacon fat and Caesar dressing contains anchovies. Make sure you check the ingredients in the dressing to make sure it is vegetarian friendly and doesn't have an animal hiding in it.

Cheese is eaten by some vegetarians but not all cheese is vegetarian! Some cheeses use animal rennet in their manufacturing, which is enzymes from animal stomachs! You will find cheeses that are vegetarian or you can ignore this fact, it is up to you. If you check the labels you will find the vegetarian cheeses are labelled as such.

If you eat tortillas then check the ingredients as many of them are made with animal products, as are many other chips. Some of the meaty flavors of chip are in fact vegetarian and typically they will be labelled so you know what you can and cannot eat.

Look out for gummy type sweets as well as usually these will contain gelatine which comes from animal bones. There are some vegetarian versions if you are being strict, though a lot of vegetarians will overlook this fact in their need for candy! Check the ingredients of Jello and marshmallows as these can also contain gelatine.

And bad news for many men here, some beers aren't entirely vegetarian as they can be clarified with something called isinglass or fish bladders. Some beers are fine, though it is up to you how strict you want to be here.

There are a lot of foods that you may think are safe to eat but are in fact not vegetarian. Take some time to read the labels and you will soon work out which foods you can and cannot eat following the above guidelines.

Vegetarian Sources of Vitamins and Protein

A vegetarian who doesn't eat the right type of diet could end up with chronic fatigue and a compromised immune system, so it is important that you eat the right types of food.

Firstly, you need to decide what type of vegetarian diet you are going to follow. A lacto-ovo vegetarian is going to get a lot of more essential nutrients than a pure vegan, but you can still be healthy when following the latter diet.

You need to understand the vitamin content of food and ensure that you eat a balanced diet that includes plenty of fruit and vegetables, as these are your primary sources of vitamins. You want around six to eight portions of vegetables and three to four of fruit every single day. If you are not getting these then you are going to become deficient in vital nutrients.

Protein is essential and it isn't hard to get the required levels on a vegetarian diet. However, you need to make sure it is coming from good sources such as tofu, beans, lentils, chickpeas and so on. You can get protein from textured vegetable proteins (meat replacements) though this is highly processed and can contain chemicals, saturated fats and other unwanted additives.

You can also get your protein from whole grains and leafy green vegetables as well as dairy products and eggs. If you are concerned about your protein levels, then you can use vegetarian protein powders mixed into smoothies or juices.

If you feel that you are lacking in the proper nutrition, then get some vitamin tablets and start taking them. You may find you are not getting enough vitamin B-12, calcium and iron but you can get iron from mushrooms, tofu and cashew nuts. If you do choose to take an iron supplement then you will need to also take a vitamin C supplement to help you absorb the iron.

Calcium is found in the leafy green vegetables as well as fortified products such as soy milk and so on. If you are taking a calcium supplement, then also take a vitamin D supplement as this will help you absorb the calcium properly.

B-12 is the big problem for pure vegans because it is found in animal products and not in vegetables. However, you can get this from fortified yeasts, cereal or soy milk. It is found in eggs and dairy products if you are a lacto-ovo vegetarian.

You will also need Omega-3 fatty acids which are vital for your brain development, eyesight and muscles. This is found in eggs but can also be found in pure vegetarian sources such as soybeans, tofu, walnuts, flaxseed oil and canola oil. If you are in doubt about how much of this you are getting then take a supplement.

When you are getting the right nutrition from your vegetarian diet you will feel fantastic and really benefit from following this way of eating. Make sure you are getting all the right vitamins and if you feel you aren't then take some supplements to give your system a boost.

Chapter 2: Breakfast

Breakfast Egg Sandwich

Preparation time: 15 minutes
Cooking time: 3 minutes
Servings: 1

Ingredients

Whole wheat bagel – 1, split

Dijon mustard – 1 tsp.

Yogurt cheese – 2 Tbsp.

Avocado – ¼, slightly mashed

Tomato – 2 to 3 slices

Alfalfa sprouts - ¼ cup

Whole egg – 1 + 2 egg whites

Pinch sea salt and black pepper

Cooking spray

Directions

First, set up oven rack about six inches from the top of oven and turn on broiler.

Toast the bagel under the broiler (cut side up).

Spread both sides of a toasted bagel with Dijon mustard and yogurt cheese. On the top half of the bagel, spread mashed avocado and add the tomato slices and sprouts.

Heat a skillet and spray with cooking spray.

Beat eggs with salt and pepper and pour into the skillet.

Cook until firm.

Arrange the eggs with the bagel and serve.

Cottage Cheese Griddlecakes

Preparation time: 5 minutes
Cooking time: 20 minutes
Servings: 14

Ingredients

Whole wheat flour – 1 ¼ cups

Baking powder – 2 tsp.

Baking soda – ½ tsp.

Unrefined sugar – 3 Tbsp.

Pinch freshly grated nutmeg

Pinch sea salt

Low-fat milk – 1 cup

Low-fat cottage cheese – 1 cup

Egg yolk – 1

Vanilla extract – 1 tsp.

Finely grated lemon zest – 1 tsp.

Egg whites – 3

Cooking spray

Directions

In a bowl, whisk together sugar, nutmeg, baking soda, baking powder, salt, and flour.

In another bowl, whisk together cottage cheese, milk, egg yolk, vanilla extract, and lemon zest.

Mix both wet and dry ingredients until just combined.

Add egg whites to a separate bowl and beat them into stiff peaks. Fold egg whites into batter.

Heat a pancake griddle and spray with cooking spray.

Scoop about 1/3 cup of batter onto the griddle for each cake and shape it into a round.

Cook about 4 to 5 minutes or until the edges are starting to dry. Then flip and cook for 1 to 2 minutes more.

Repeat with the remaining batter.

Serve.

Amaranth Oat Waffles

Preparation time: 15 minutes
Cooking time: 15 minutes
Servings: 14

Dry ingredients

Whole grain amaranth flour – 1 cup

Oat flour – ½ cup

Oat bran – ½ cup

Whole soy flour – ½ cup

Whole grain corn flour – ½ cup

Whole grain coarse cornmeal – ¼ cup

Flax meal – 2 Tbsp.

Baking powder – 2 ½ tsp.

Baking soda – ½ tsp.

Pinch sea salt

Wet ingredients

Equal parts of soy or almond milk – 2 ½ cups

Egg – 1 plus 2 egg whites

Unrefined sugar – ¼ cup

Vanilla extract – 1 tsp.

Cooking spray

Directions

Preheat waffle iron and grease it.

In a bowl, whisk the dry ingredients. In another bowl, whisk together the wet ingredients. Mix both wet and dry ingredients until just moistened.

Pour enough batter to cover cooking area. Close the lid.

Cook until waffle releases from iron.

Repeat with the remaining batter and serve.

Blueberry Baked Oatmeal

Preparation time: 10 minutes
Cooking time: 20 minutes
Servings: 5

Ingredients

Cooking spray

Unsweetened soy, rice, or almond milk – 1 cup

Whole egg – 1, plus 2 egg whites

Unsweetened applesauce – ½ cup

Pure maple syrup – 2 Tbsp.

Vanilla extract – ½ tsp.

Baking powder – 1 tsp.

Ground cinnamon – 1 tsp.

Freshly grated nutmeg – 1 pinch

Sea salt – 1 pinch

Old-fashioned rolled oats – 2 ½ cups

Oat bran – ¼ cup

Chopped pecans – ½ cup

Frozen or fresh blueberries – 1 ½ cups, divided

Directions

Preheat the oven to 350F.

Coat a 3-quart casserole dish with cooking spray.

Whisk together egg, egg whites, milk, applesauce, maple syrup, vanilla, baking powder, cinnamon, sea salt, and nutmeg.

Mix in oat bran, oats, and pecans.

Gently fold in half of the blueberries. Scatter remaining blueberries across the bottom of the casserole dish.

Scrape oatmeal mixture into a casserole dish and bake, uncovered, for 35 to 40 minutes, or until golden brown around the edges.

French Toast with Strawberries

Preparation time: 20 minutes
Cooking time: 5 to 7 minutes
Servings: 6

Ingredients

Firm tofu – 1 (12 oz.) package

Unsweetened soy, rice or almond milk – ½ cup

Pure maple syrup – 2 tsp.

Pure vanilla extract – 1 tsp.

Almond extract – ½ tsp.

Ground cinnamon – ½ tsp.

Pinch sea salt

Coconut oil – 2 Tbsp.

Whole grain bread – 6 slices

Sliced fresh strawberries – 1 ½ cups

Sliced almonds – 6 Tbsp.

Directions

To a blender, add the batter and blend until combined well. Pour into a bowl.

Heat a skillet

Then grease with oil.

Dip a slice of bread in batter, then turn it over and dip again to soak completely.

Place on the griddle and repeat until the griddle is covered with battered bread.

Sauté bread until the griddle is covered with battered bread.

Sauté bread until cooked through and browned, 2 to 3 minutes per side.

Top bread slices with sliced strawberries and almonds and serve.

Dark and Addictive Bran Muffins

Preparation time: 5 minutes
Cooking time: 20 minutes
Servings: 15

Ingredients

Cooking spray

Boiling water – 1 cup

Wheat bran – 1 cup

Wet ingredients

Coconut oil – 2 Tbsp. melted

Unrefined sugar – ¼ cup

Unsulfured blackstrap molasses

Unsweetened applesauce – ½ cup

Soy, rice or almond milk – 1 cup

Plain soy yogurt – 1 cup

Orange zest – 1 Tbsp.

Dry ingredients

Whole wheat flour – 2 ½ cups

Whole grain soy flour – 2 Tbsp.

Flax meal – 2 Tbsp.

Baking soda – 2 ½ tsp.

Sea salt – ¼ tsp.

All-natural, whole-grain bran flake cereal – 2 cups

Flaxseed for garnish

Directions

Keep the oven rack in the center.

Preheat to 400F.

Prepare a muffin tin by lining with cooking spray.

Pour boiling water over bran and set aside.

Whisk together wet ingredients until combined well.

In a bowl, whisk together dry ingredients until combined well. Add wet ingredients and mix. Add bran flake cereal and bran and water mixture, stir to combine.

Divide batter among 15 muffin cups and sprinkle the tops with flaxseeds.

Bake for 20 minutes.

Remove from the oven, cool and serve.

Brown Rice Breakfast

Preparation time: 5 minutes
Cooking time: 10 minutes
Servings: 2

Ingredients

Cooked brown rice – 2 cups

Unsweetened almond or soy milk – 2 cups

Sliced raw almonds – ¼ cup

Flaxseed – 1 Tbsp.

Maple syrup – 2 tsp. divided

Pinch of grated nutmeg

Directions

Divide rice between two bowls and add half of the milk and remaining ingredients to each.

Serve.

Smoothie on the Beach

Preparation time: 10 minutes
Cooking time: 0 minutes
Servings: 3

Ingredients

Soy yogurt – 2 cups

Frozen mango, pineapple chunks, strawberries, and peach slices

Hulled hem seeds – 1 Tbsp.

Golden flaxseed – 1 Tbsp.

Oat bran – 1 Tbsp.

Vegan protein powder – 2 Tbsp.

Pure vanilla extract – ½ tsp.

Juice of 1 lime

Directions

Place all ingredients in a blender

Blend until smooth.

Serve.

Buttermilk Bran Pancakes

Preparation time: 10 minutes
Cooking time: 10 minutes
Servings: 4

Ingredients

High-fiber wheat bran cereal – 1/3 cup

Buttermilk – 1 ¼ cup

Egg – 1

Brown sugar – 2 Tbsp. packed

Vegetable oil – 2 tsp.

All-purpose flour – 1 cup

Baking powder – 1 tsp.

Baking soda - -1/2 tsp.

Salt – ¼ tsp.

Chopped apple – ¼ cup

Coarsely chopped walnuts – ¼ cup

Sugar – 1 Tbsp.

Ground cinnamon – ¼ tsp.

Yogurt – 1/3 cup

Cooking spray and ground cinnamon

Directions

Place the cereal in a medium bowl. Add oil, brown sugar, egg, and buttermilk. Stir and mix well. Set aside for 10 minutes.

Meanwhile, in a small bowl, stir together baking soda, baking powder, flour, and salt. Sat aside.

For the topping: In another bowl, add walnuts and apple. Combine ¼ ts: cinnamon and sugar. Then toss with apple mixture. Stir yogurt to make it creamy. Then add on top of apple mixture.

Add flour mixture to the buttermilk mixture. Stir until combined.

Coat a pan with cooking spray.

Then heat on medium-low heat.

Pour ¼ cup of batter into the hot pan for each pancake. Cook until the bottom is golden, about 1 to 2 minutes, then flip and cook until golden, about 1 minute more.

Transfer to a serving plate.

Serve with apple-walnut topping and sprinkle with more cinnamon if desired.

Mexican Tomatillo-Poblano Eggs

Preparation time: 10 minutes
Cooking time: 5 minutes
Servings: 6

Ingredients

Fresh tomatillos – 2 pounds, husked and chopped

Fresh Poblano Chile peppers - 1 ½ cups (seeded and chopped)

Chopped onion – ½ cup

Fresh Serrano Chile pepper – 1 Tbsp. (seeded and finely chopped)

Garlic cloves – 2, minced

Ground cumin – 1 ½ tsp.

Dried oregano – 1 tsp. crushed

Salt – ½ tsp.

Ground coriander – ½ tsp.

Tortilla chips – ½ cup

Fresh cilantro – ¼ cup

Lime juice – 2 Tbsp.

Eggs – 6

Monterey Jack or Shredded Chihuahua Cheese – ¾ cup

Chili powder as needed

Directions

Combine first nine ingredients (through coriander) in a slow cooker.

Cook on high for 3 to 3 ½ minutes or low on 6 to 7 minute s.

Then turn the heat to high cooking on low.

Stir in cilantro, lime juice, and tortilla chips. Into a custard cup, break an egg and slip the egg into the tomato mixture. Repeat with the remaining eggs.

Cover and cook until eggs are cooked about 25 to 35 minutes.

Top servings with cilantro, chili powder, and cheese.

Serve with tortilla chips.

Vegetable Cheese Strata
Preparation time: Overnight

Cooking time: 25 minutes
Servings: 8

Ingredients

Nonstick cooking spray

Cubed Whole wheat French bread – 5 cups

Olive oil – 4 tsp.

Chopped onion – 1 cup

Chopped red sweet pepper – 1 cup

Garlic – 4 cloves, minced

Fresh Cremini Mushrooms – 2 cups, sliced

Lightly packed fresh spinach leaves – 3 cups

Shredded part-skim mozzarella cheese – 1 cup

Finely Shredded Parmesan cheese – 1/3 cup

Eggs – 8

Egg whites – 8

Fat-free milk – 1 ¾ cups

Dijon-style mustard – 1 Tbsp.

Salt – ½ tsp.

Black pepper – ½ tsp.

Directions

Lightly coat a baking dish (3-qt) with cooking spray.
Then spread half of the bread cubes in it.

Heat 2 tsp. olive oil skillet. Add garlic, sweet pepper,
onion and cook until tender. Stirring occasionally.
Remove from skillet.

Add 2 tsp. oil to the skillet. Then add mushrooms. Cook
and stir until tender. Add spinach and cook until slightly
wilted. Stir in the onion mixture.

In a small bowl, mix both cheeses and reserve 1/3 cup.

Spread half of the vegetable mixture over bread cubes
in the dish. Sprinkle with remaining cheese mixture.

Layer with vegetable mixture and remaining bread cubes.

Whisk together the remaining ingredients in a large bowl. Then pour over the dish (on top of the mixture). Cover and chill overnight.

Preheat the oven to 325F. Bake, uncovered, for 45 minutes. Sprinkle with reserved 1/3 cup cheese mixture.

Bake for 5 to 10 minutes. Cool for 10 minutes before serving.

Creamy Fruit-Filled Crepes

Preparation time: 10 minutes
Cooking time: 10 minutes
Servings: 4

Ingredients

Egg – 1, lightly beaten

Fat-free milk – ¾ cup

All-purpose flour – ½ cup

Olive oil-1 Tbsp.

Salt – 1/8 tsp.

Desired topping

Directions

In a bowl, whisk together oil, salt, flour, milk, and egg until smooth.

Lightly grease a nonstick skillet and heat over medium heat.

Then remove the pan from the stove and add 2 Tbsp. batter. Tilt the batter to spread evenly.

Return to heat and cook until browned on the bottom, about 1 to 2 minutes. Remove and place on paper towels. Repeat with the remaining batter.

To assemble, place crepes on the serving plate (browned side down). Spoon desired filling onto half of each crepe, then fold.

Serve.

Breakfast Tacos

Preparation time: 10 minutes
Cooking time: 20 minutes
Servings: 4

Ingredients

Corn tortillas -6 inches

Vegetable oil – 1 tsp.

Salt – ¼ tsp.

Shredded hash brown potatoes – 1 cup, frozen

Chopped green sweet pepper – 2 Tbsp.

Eggs – 4, lightly beaten

Egg whites – 2

Salsa – 5 Tbsp.

Reduced sodium black beans – ½ cup, drained and rinsed

Shredded reduced-fat cheddar cheese – ¼ cup

Lime wedges and salsa

Directions

Place rack in the middle and preheat the oven to 375F.

Stack tortillas and wrap in damp paper towels. Microwave on high until softened and warm, about 40 seconds.

Brush both sides of the tortillas with oil and sprinkle with salt. Arrange the tortillas on the oven rack and bake until crisp, about 7 minutes. Transfer to a plate.

Meanwhile, coat a skillet with cooking spray and heat over medium heat.

Add sweet pepper and hash brown potatoes and cook until potatoes are light brown, about 2 to 3 minutes. Stirring occasionally.

In a small bowl, combine 1 Tbsp. salsa, egg whites, and eggs. Then pour the mixture over the potato mixture in the pan.

Cook, until the mixture starts to set, don't stir.

Then tilt the pan and/or lift the mixture with a spatula, so the uncooked portion gets cooked.

Continue to cook until the mixture is cooked completely, about 2 to 3 minutes more. Remove from the heat when cooked.

Add egg mixture into tortilla shells. Top with 4 Tbsp. salsa and beans. Sprinkle with cheese.

Serve with additional salsa and lime wedges.

Rice and Bean Frittata
Preparation time: 10 minutes
Cooking time: 20 minutes
Servings: 4

Ingredients

Vegetable oil – 2 Tbsp.

Sliced zucchini – 2 cups

Cooked long grain and wild rice – 1 (8.8 ounces) pouch

Garbanzo, or navy beans – 1 (15-ounce can), rinsed and drained

Eggs – 6, lightly beaten

Milk – ¼ cup

Salt – ¼ tsp.

Ground black pepper – ¼ tsp.

Shredded Colby and Monterey Jack Cheese – 1 cup

Cherry tomatoes or fresh parsley

Directions

Heat oil in a large skillet.

Add zucchini to the skillet. Cook and stir until crisp-tender.

Microwave rice according to package directions. Add the beans and rice in the skillet. Stir to combine.

In a bowl, combine milk, salt, pepper, and eggs. Then pour in the skillet over the rice mixture. Cook over medium heat.

Gently lift the edges to cook the mixture evenly. Cook until the mixture is set.

Sprinkle with cheese. Top with parsley and cherry tomatoes.

Serve.

Breakfast Pita Pizzas

Preparation time: 10 minutes
Cooking time: 20 minutes
Servings: 2

Ingredients

Olive oil – 1 tsp.

Sliced fresh mushrooms – ½ cup

Chopped red and green sweet pepper - ½ cup

Firm tub-style tofu – 3 ounces, drained and crumbled

Thinly sliced green onion – 2 Tbsp.

Garlic – 1 clove, minced

Ground black pepper – 1/8 tsp.

Whole wheat pita bread round – 1, split in half
horizontally

Shredded reduced-fat cheddar cheese – ½ cup

Refrigerated fresh salsa – 1 cup

Directions

Preheat the oven to 375F.

Heat oil in a skillet.

Add sweet pepper and mushrooms and cook until
tender, about 5 to 8 minutes. Stirring occasionally. Stir
in black pepper, garlic, green onion, and tofu.

Place pita halves on a baking sheet cut sides down.

Sprinkle with ¼ cup of the cheese, then top with
mushroom mixture. Then sprinkle with the rest of ¼-
cup cheese.

Bake until heated through and cheese is melted about 8 to 10 minutes.

Cool, slice, and serve with salsa.

Waffle Sandwiches

Preparation time: 10 minutes
Cooking time: 10 minutes
Servings: 4

Ingredients

Light cream cheese – ½ cup, softened

Honey – 4 tsp.

Whole grain sandwich bread – 8 slices

Sliced fresh strawberries – 1 ½ cups

Low-fat granola – ¼ cup

Salted – 2 Tbsp. roasted sunflower kernels

Nonstick cooking spray and honey

Directions

Combine 4 tsp. honey and cream cheese in a small bowl. Spread cream cheese on one side of the bread slices.

Top four of the bread slices with sunflower kernels.

Then with granola, and strawberries.

Then top with the remaining four bread slices, spread sides down.

Coat a waffle baker with cooking spray and heat according to instructions.

One at a time, cook the sandwiches in the waffle bake until golden, about 2 minutes.

Remove with a fork when cooked.

Cut serve with additional honey.

Peanut Butter and Fruit Quinoa

Preparation time: 10 minutes
Cooking time: 15 minutes
Servings: 4

Ingredients

Water – 2 cups

Quinoa – 1 cup

Apple juice or cider – ¼ cup

Reduced-fat creamy peanut butter – 3 Tbsp.

Banana – 1 small, chopped

Raspberry or strawberry – 2 Tbsp.

Unsalted, blanched peanuts – 4 tsp.

Directions

Combine water and quinoa in a pan. Bring to a boil. Reduce heat to medium and cook until water is absorbed, about 10 to 15 minutes. Remove from heat. Add peanut butter and apple juice. Stir until combined. Stir in banana.

Divide mixture among bowls. Top each bowl with fruit and peanuts.

Serve.

Easy Huevos Rancheros

Preparation time: 10 minutes
Cooking time: 10 to 15 minutes
Servings: 1

Ingredients

Vegetable oil – 1 Tbsp.

Tortilla wrap – 1 corn

Egg – 1

Black beans – 200g can, drained

Juice of ½ lime

Ripe avocado – ½, peeled and sliced

Feta – 50g, crumbled

Hot chili sauce as needed

Directions

In a frying pan, heat oil over high heat.

Add the tortilla and fry until crisping at the edges, about 1 to 2 minutes on each side. Transfer to a plate.

Crack and add the eggs and cook as you like.

Meanwhile, tip the beans in a bowl. Add a squeeze of lime and season. Then lightly mash with a fork.

Spread the beans over the tortilla. Top with feta, avocado, egg and chili sauce.

Squeeze with a little juice and serve.

Oat Flour Pancakes
Preparation time: 10 minutes
Cooking time: 10 minutes
Servings: 5

Ingredients

Unsweetened applesauce – ½ cup

Oat flour rolled oats – 1 ¼ cup (ground in a blender)

Non-dairy milk – ½ cup

Lemon juice – 2 tsp.

Maple syrup – 2 Tbsp.

Baking powder – 1 tsp.

Baking soda – 1 tsp.

Vanilla extract – 1 tsp.

Directions

Combine everything in a blender.

Blend until combined, don't over blend.

Heat a non-stick skillet over medium heat.

Add 1/3 cup batter in the pan.

Then spread into a circle.

Cook for 2 to 3 minutes.

Then flip and cook another 2 to 3 minutes.

Repeat to finish.

Top with maple syrup, hemp seeds, and fruit.

Chapter 3: Salads and dressings

Artichoke and Green Olives with Walnut Vinaigrette

Preparation time: 10 minutes
Cooking time: 0 minutes
Servings: 5

Ingredients:

1 artichoke, rinsed & patted

½ cup green olives

Dressing

2 tbsp. red wine vinegar

4 tablespoons extra virgin olive oil

Freshly ground black pepper

3/4 cup finely coarsely ground walnuts

Sea salt

Combine all of the dressing ingredients in a food processor.

Toss with the rest of the ingredients and combine well.

Endive with Black Olives and Artichoke Hearts

Ingredients:

1 head Endive, rinsed, patted and shredded

½ cup black olives

½ cup artichoke hearts

Dressing

2 tbsp. apple cider vinegar

4 tablespoons olive oil

Freshly ground black pepper

3/4 cup finely ground almonds

Sea salt

Combine all of the dressing ingredients in a food processor.

Toss with the rest of the ingredients and combine well.

Swiss Chard and Artichoke Hearts with Black Olive Salad

Preparation time: 10 minutes
Cooking time: 0 minutes
Servings: 5

Ingredients:

1 head Swiss chard, rinsed, patted and shredded

½ cup black olives

½ cup artichoke hearts

Dressing

2 tbsp. white wine vinegar

4 tablespoons extra virgin olive oil

Freshly ground black pepper

3/4 cup finely ground peanuts

Sea salt

Combine all of the dressing ingredients in a food processor.

Toss with the rest of the ingredients and combine well.

Collard Greens Black Olive and Artichoke Heart Salad

Preparation time: 10 minutes
Cooking time: 0 minutes
Servings: 5

Ingredients:

1 bunch collard greens, rinsed, patted and shredded

½ cup black olives

½ cup artichoke hearts

Dressing

2 tbsp. red wine vinegar

4 tablespoons extra virgin olive oil

Freshly ground black pepper

3/4 cup finely ground almonds

Sea salt

Combine all of the dressing ingredients in a food processor.

Toss with the rest of the ingredients and combine well.

Heart with Macadamia Vinaigrette Salad

Preparation time: 10 minutes
Cooking time: 0 minutes
Servings: 5

Ingredients:

1 head romaine lettuce, rinsed, patted and shredded

½ cup black olives

½ cup artichoke hearts

Dressing

2 tbsp. balsamic vinegar

4 tablespoons macadamia oil

Freshly ground black pepper

3/4 cup finely coarsely ground cashews

Sea salt

Combine all of the dressing ingredients in a food processor.

Toss with the rest of the ingredients and combine well.

Bib Lettuce Black Olives and Artichoke Heart Salad

Preparation time: 10 minutes
Cooking time: 0 minutes
Servings: 5

Ingredients:

1 head bib lettuce, rinsed, patted and shredded

½ cup black olives

½ cup artichoke hearts

Dressing

2 tbsp. white wine vinegar

4 tablespoons extra virgin olive oil

Freshly ground black pepper

3/4 cup finely ground almonds

Sea salt

Combine all of the dressing ingredients in a food processor.

Toss with the rest of the ingredients and combine well.

Boston Lettuce with *Black* Olive Salad

Preparation time: 10 minutes
Cooking time: 0 minutes
Servings: 5

Ingredients:

1 head Boston lettuce, rinsed, patted and shredded

½ cup black olives

½ cup artichoke hearts

Dressing

2 tbsp. apple cider vinegar

4 tablespoons extra virgin olive oil

Freshly ground black pepper

3/4 cup finely ground peanuts

Sea salt

Combine all of the dressing ingredients in a food processor.

Toss with the rest of the ingredients and combine well.

Romaine Lettuce with Artichoke Heart and Cashew Vinaigrette Salad

Preparation time: 10 minutes
Cooking time: 0 minutes
Servings: 5

Ingredients:

1 head romaine lettuce, rinsed, patted and shredded

½ cup black olives

½ cup artichoke hearts

Dressing

2 tbsp. red wine vinegar

4 tablespoons olive oil

Freshly ground black pepper

3/4 cup finely coarsely ground cashews

Sea salt

Combine all of the dressing ingredients in a food processor.

Toss with the rest of the ingredients and combine well.

Mustard Greens Artichoke Heart and Green Olive Salad

Preparation time: 10 minutes
Cooking time: 0 minutes
Servings: 5

Ingredients:

1 bunch of mustard greens, rinsed, patted and shredded

½ cup green olives

½ cup artichoke hearts

Dressing

2 tbsp. red wine vinegar

4 tablespoons macadamia oil

Freshly ground black pepper

3/4 cup finely coarsely ground walnuts

Sea salt

Combine all of the dressing ingredients in a food processor.

Toss with the rest of the ingredients and combine well.

Beetroot Kalamata Olives and Artichoke Heart Salad

Preparation time: 10 minutes
Cooking time: 0 minutes
Servings: 5

Ingredients:

2 beetroots, peeled and sliced lengthwise

½ cup Kalamata olives

½ cup artichoke hearts

Dressing

2 tbsp. white wine vinegar

4 tablespoons extra virgin olive oil

Freshly ground black pepper

3/4 cup finely ground almonds

Sea salt

Combine all of the dressing ingredients in a food processor.

Toss with the rest of the ingredients and combine well.

Collard Greens Baby Corn and Artichoke Heart Salad

Preparation time: 10 minutes
Cooking time: 0 minutes
Servings: 5

Ingredients:

1 bunch of collard greens, rinsed, patted and shredded

½ cup baby corn

½ cup artichoke hearts

Dressing

2 tbsp. balsamic vinegar

4 tablespoons macadamia oil

Freshly ground black pepper

3/4 cup finely coarsely ground cashews

Sea salt

Combine all of the dressing ingredients in a food processor.

Toss with the rest of the ingredients and combine well.

Boston Lettuce Baby Carrots and Artichoke Heart Salad

Preparation time: 10 minutes
Cooking time: 0 minutes
Servings: 5

Ingredients:

1 head Boston lettuce, rinsed , patted and shredded

½ cup baby carrots

½ cup artichoke hearts

Dressing

2 tbsp. white wine vinegar

4 tablespoons extra virgin olive oil

Freshly ground black pepper

3/4 cup finely ground peanuts

Sea salt

Combine all of the dressing ingredients in a food processor.

Toss with the rest of the ingredients and combine well.

Kale Black Olives and Baby Corn Salad

Preparation time: 10 minutes
Cooking time: 0 minutes
Servings: 5

Ingredients:

1 bunch of kale, rinsed, patted and shredded

½ cup black olives

½ cup canned baby corn

Dressing

2 tbsp. apple cider vinegar

4 tablespoons olive oil

Freshly ground black pepper

3/4 cup finely ground almonds

Sea salt

Combine all of the dressing ingredients in a food processor.

Toss with the rest of the ingredients and combine well.

Romaine Lettuce & Baby Carrots with Walnut Vinaigrette Salad

Preparation time: 10 minutes
Cooking time: 0 minutes
Servings: 5

Ingredients:

1 bunch of kale, rinsed, patted and shredded

½ cup black olives

½ cup baby carrots

Dressing

2 tbsp. white wine vinegar

4 tablespoons extra virgin olive oil

Freshly ground black pepper

3/4 cup finely coarsely ground walnuts

Sea salt

Combine all of the dressing ingredients in a food processor.

Toss with the rest of the ingredients and combine well.

Boston Lettuce with Capers and Artichoke Heart Salad

Preparation time: 10 minutes
Cooking time: 0 minutes
Servings: 5

Ingredients:

1 bunch of mustard greens

½ cup capers

½ cup artichoke hearts

Dressing

2 tbsp. red wine vinegar

4 tablespoons extra virgin olive oil

Freshly ground black pepper

3/4 cup finely ground almonds

Sea salt

Combine all of the dressing ingredients in a food processor.

Toss with the rest of the ingredients and combine well.

Bib Lettuce Olive and Baby Carrot with Walnut Vinaigrette Salad

Preparation time: 10 minutes
Cooking time: 0 minutes
Servings: 5

Ingredients:

1 head bib lettuce, rinsed, patted and shredded

½ cup black olives

½ cup baby carrots

Dressing

2 tbsp. apple cider vinegar

4 tablespoons extra virgin olive oil

Freshly ground black pepper

3/4 cup finely coarsely ground walnuts

Sea salt

Combine all of the dressing ingredients in a food processor.

Toss with the rest of the ingredients and combine well.

Collard Greens with Baby Corn Salad

Preparation time: 15 minutes
Cooking time: 0 minutes
Servings: 5

Ingredients:

1 bunch of collard greens

½ cup black olives

½ cup canned baby corn

Dressing

2 tbsp. red wine vinegar

4 tablespoons extra virgin olive oil

Freshly ground black pepper

3/4 cup finely ground almonds

Sea salt

Combine all of the dressing ingredients in a food processor.

Toss with the rest of the ingredients and combine well.

Boston Lettuce Red Onion and Artichoke Heart with Peanut Vinaigrette Salad

Preparation time: 10 minutes
Cooking time: 0 minutes
Servings: 5

Ingredients:

1 head Boston lettuce, rinsed, patted and shredded

½ cup chopped red onion

½ cup artichoke hearts

5 ounces cream cheese, crumbled

Dressing

2 tbsp. white wine vinegar

4 tablespoons extra virgin olive oil

Freshly ground black pepper

3/4 cup finely ground peanuts

Sea salt

Combine all of the dressing ingredients in a food processor.

Toss with the rest of the ingredients and combine well.

Bib Lettuce Black Olives and Baby Corn with Almond Vinaigrette Salad

Preparation time: 10 minutes
Cooking time: 0 minutes
Servings: 5

Ingredients:

1 head Bib lettuce, rinsed, patted and shredded

½ cup black olives

½ cup canned baby corn

Dressing

2 tbsp. white wine vinegar

4 tablespoons olive oil

Freshly ground black pepper

3/4 cup finely ground almonds

Sea salt

Combine all of the dressing ingredients in a food processor.

Toss with the rest of the ingredients and combine well.

Endive and Green Olive Salad

Preparation time: 10 minutes
Cooking time: 0 minutes
Servings: 5

Ingredients:

1 endives rinsed, patted and shredded

½ cup green olives

½ cup artichoke hearts

Dressing

2 tbsp. white wine vinegar

4 tablespoons macadamia oil

Freshly ground black pepper

3/4 cup finely coarsely ground cashews

Sea salt

Combine all of the dressing ingredients in a food processor.

Toss with the rest of the ingredients and combine well.

Mixed Greens Olives and Artichoke Heart Salad

Preparation time: 10 minutes
Cooking time: 0 minutes
Servings: 5

Ingredients:

1 bunch of mixed greens, rinsed, patted and shredded

½ cup black olives

½ cup artichoke hearts

Dressing

2 tbsp. white wine vinegar

4 tablespoons extra virgin olive oil

Freshly ground black pepper

3/4 cup finely coarsely ground walnuts

Sea salt

Combine all of the dressing ingredients in a food processor.

Toss with the rest of the ingredients and combine well.

Iceberg Lettuce and Artichoke Heart Salad

Preparation time: 10 minutes
Cooking time: 0 minutes
Servings: 5

Ingredients:

1 head Iceberg lettuce, rinsed, patted and shredded

½ cup Kalamata olives

½ cup artichoke hearts

5 ounces ricotta cheese

Dressing

2 tbsp. balsamic vinegar

4 tablespoons extra virgin olive oil

Freshly ground black pepper

3/4 cup finely ground almonds

Sea salt

Combine all of the dressing ingredients in a food processor.

Toss with the rest of the ingredients and combine well.

Artichoke Capers and Artichoke Heart Salad

Preparation time: 10 minutes
Cooking time: 0 minutes
Servings: 5

Ingredients:

1 artichoke, rinsed, patted and shredded

½ cup capers

½ cup artichoke hearts

Dressing

2 tbsp. white wine vinegar

4 tablespoons extra virgin olive oil

Freshly ground black pepper

3/4 cup finely ground almonds

Sea salt

Combine all of the dressing ingredients in a food processor.

Toss with the rest of the ingredients and combine well.

Mixed Greens Baby Corn and Artichoke Heart Salad

Preparation time: 10 minutes
Cooking time: 0 minutes
Servings: 5

Ingredients:

1 bunch Mesclun, rinsed, patted and shredded

½ cup canned baby corn

½ cup artichoke hearts

Dressing

2 tbsp. white wine vinegar

4 tablespoons extra virgin olive oil

Freshly ground black pepper

3/4 cup finely ground peanuts

Sea salt

Combine all of the dressing ingredients in a food processor.

Toss with the rest of the ingredients and combine well.

Bib Lettuce with Tomatillo Dressing

Preparation time: 10 minutes
Cooking time: 0 minutes
Servings: 5

Ingredients:

1 head Bib lettuce, shredded

4 large tomatoes, seeded and chopped

4 radishes, thinly sliced

Dressing

6 tomatillos, rinsed and halved

1 jalapeno, halved

1 white onion, quartered

2 tablespoons extra virgin olive oil

Kosher salt and freshly ground black pepper

1/2 teaspoon ground cumin

1 cup Dairy free cream cheese

2 tablespoons fresh lemon juice

Preheat the oven to 400 degrees F.

For the dressing, place the tomatillos, jalapeno and onion on a cookie sheet.

Drizzle with olive oil and sprinkle with salt and pepper.

Roast in the oven for 25-30 min. until vegetables begin to brown and slightly darken.

Transfer to a food processor and let it cool then blend.

Add the rest of the ingredients and refrigerate for an minute .

Toss with the rest of the ingredients and combine well.

Enoki Mushroom and Cucumber Salad

Preparation time: 10 minutes
Cooking time: 0 minutes
Servings: 5

Ingredients:

15 Enoki Mushrooms, thinly sliced

1/4 white onion, peeled, halved lengthwise, and thinly sliced

1 large cucumber, halved lengthwise and thinly sliced

Dressing

¼ cup extra-virgin olive oil

2 splashes white wine vinegar

Coarse salt and black pepper

Combine all of the dressing ingredients.

Toss with the rest of the ingredients and combine well.

Tomato and Zucchini Salad

Preparation time: 10 minutes
Cooking time: 0 minutes
Servings: 5

Ingredients:

1/4 white onion, peeled, halved lengthwise, and thinly sliced

1 large Zucchini halved lengthwise ,thinly sliced & blanched

5 ounces mozarella cheese, shredded

Dressing

¼ cup extra-virgin olive oil

2 tbsp. apple cider vinegar

Coarse salt and black pepper

Combine all of the dressing ingredients.

Toss with the rest of the ingredients and combine well.

Tomatillos with Cucumber and Ricotta Cheese Salad

Ingredients:

10 Tomatillos, halved lengthwise, seeded, and thinly sliced

1/4 white onion, peeled, halved lengthwise, and thinly sliced

1 large cucumber, halved lengthwise and thinly sliced

5 ounces ricotta cheese

Dressing

¼ cup extra-virgin olive oil

2 splashes white wine vinegar

Coarse salt and black pepper

Combine all of the dressing ingredients.

Toss with the rest of the ingredients and combine well.

Plum Tomato and Onion Salad

Preparation time: 10 minutes
Cooking time: 0 minutes
Servings: 5

Ingredients:

1/4 white onion, peeled, halved lengthwise, and thinly sliced

1 large cucumber, halved lengthwise and thinly sliced

Dressing

¼ cup extra-virgin olive oil

2 tbsp. apple cider vinegar

Coarse salt and black pepper

Prep

Combine all of the dressing ingredients.

Toss with the rest of the ingredients and combine well.

Zucchini Pepperjack Cheese and Tomato Salad

Preparation time: 20 minutes
Cooking time: 0 minutes
Servings: 5

Ingredients:

1/4 white onion, peeled, halved lengthwise, and thinly sliced

1 large Zucchini halved lengthwise ,thinly sliced and blanched

5 ounces pepperjack cheese, shredded

Dressing

¼ cup extra-virgin olive oil

2 splashes white wine vinegar

Coarse salt and black pepper

Combine all of the dressing ingredients.

Toss with the rest of the ingredients and combine well.

Heirloom Tomato Salad

Preparation time: 20 minutes
Cooking time: 0 minutes
Servings: 5

Ingredients:

3 Heirloom tomatoes, halved lengthwise, seeded, and thinly sliced

1/4 white onion, peeled, halved lengthwise, and thinly sliced

1 large cucumber, halved lengthwise and thinly sliced

Dressing

¼ cup extra-virgin olive oil

2 splashes white wine vinegar

Coarse salt and black pepper

Combine all of the dressing ingredients.

Toss with the rest of the ingredients and combine well.

Enoki Mushroom and Feta Cheese Salad

Preparation time: 20 minutes
Cooking time: 0 minutes
Servings: 5

Ingredients:

15 Enoki Mushrooms, thinly sliced

1/4 white onion, peeled, halved lengthwise, and thinly sliced

1 large cucumber, halved lengthwise and thinly sliced

5 ounces feta cheese, crumbled

Dressing

¼ cup extra-virgin olive oil

2 tbsp. apple cider vinegar

Coarse salt and black pepper

Combine all of the dressing ingredients.

Toss with the rest of the ingredients and combine well.

Artichoke Heart and Plum Tomato Salad

Preparation time: 20 minutes
Cooking time: 0 minutes
Servings: 5

Ingredients:

6 Artichoke Hearts (Canned)

1/4 white onion, peeled, halved lengthwise, and thinly sliced

1 large cucumber, halved lengthwise and thinly sliced

Dressing

¼ cup extra-virgin olive oil

2 splashes white wine vinegar

Coarse salt and black pepper

Combine all of the dressing ingredients.

Toss with the rest of the ingredients and combine well.

Baby Corn and Plum Tomato Salad

Preparation time: 20 minutes
Cooking time: 0 minutes
Servings: 5

Ingredients:

½ cup canned baby corn

1/4 white onion, peeled, halved lengthwise, and thinly sliced

1 large Zucchini halved lengthwise ,thinly sliced and blanched

5 ounces cream cheese, crumbled

Dressing

¼ cup extra-virgin olive oil

2 splashes white wine vinegar

Coarse salt and black pepper

Combine all of the dressing ingredients.

Toss with the rest of the ingredients and combine well.

Mixed Greens Feta Cheese and Tomato Salad

Preparation time: 15 minutes
Cooking time: 0 minutes
Servings: 4

Ingredients:

1 bunch Meslcun, rinsed and drained

1/4 white onion, peeled, halved lengthwise, and thinly sliced

1 large cucumber, halved lengthwise and thinly sliced

5 ounces feta cheese, crumbled

Dressing

¼ cup extra-virgin olive oil

2 tbsp. apple cider vinegar

Coarse salt and black pepper

Combine all of the dressing ingredients.

Toss with the rest of the ingredients and combine well.

Artichoke and Tomato Salad

Preparation time: 15 minutes
Cooking time: 0 minutes
Servings: 4

Ingredients:

1 Artichoke, rinsed and drained

1/4 white onion, peeled, halved lengthwise, and thinly sliced

1 large Zucchini halved lengthwise ,thinly sliced and blanched

Dressing

¼ cup extra-virgin olive oil

2 splashes white wine vinegar

Coarse salt and black pepper

Combine all of the dressing ingredients.

Toss with the rest of the ingredients and combine well.

Spinach and Heirloom Tomato Salad

Preparation time: 15 minutes
Cooking time: 0 minutes
Servings: 4

Ingredients:

1 bunch Spinach, rinsed and drained

3 Heirloom tomatoes, halved lengthwise, seeded, and thinly sliced

1/4 white onion, peeled, halved lengthwise, and thinly sliced

1 large cucumber, halved lengthwise and thinly sliced

Dressing

¼ cup extra-virgin olive oil

2 tbsp. apple cider vinegar

Coarse salt and black pepper

Combine all of the dressing ingredients.

Toss with the rest of the ingredients and combine well.

Mesclun and Tomatillo Salad

Preparation time: 15 minutes
Cooking time: 0 minutes
Servings: 4

Ingredients:

1 bunch Mesclun, rinsed and drained

10 Tomatillos, halved lengthwise, seeded, and thinly sliced

1/4 white onion, peeled, halved lengthwise, and thinly sliced

1 large cucumber, halved lengthwise and thinly sliced

5 ounces cottage cheese

Dressing

¼ cup extra-virgin olive oil

2 splashes white wine vinegar

Coarse salt and black pepper

Combine all of the dressing ingredients.

Toss with the rest of the ingredients and combine well.

Mesclun and Enoki Mushroom Salad

Preparation time: 15 minutes
Cooking time: 0 minutes
Servings: 4

Ingredients:

1 bunch Meslcun, rinsed and drained

15 Enoki Mushrooms, thinly sliced

1/4 white onion, peeled, halved lengthwise, and thinly sliced

1 large cucumber, halved lengthwise and thinly sliced

5 ounces ricotta cheese

Dressing

¼ cup extra-virgin olive oil

2 splashes white wine vinegar

Coarse salt and black pepper

Combine all of the dressing ingredients.

Toss with the rest of the ingredients and combine well.

Bib Lettuce and Cucumber Salad

Preparation time: 15 minutes
Cooking time: 0 minutes
Servings: 4

Ingredients:

1 bunch Bib Lettuce, rinsed and drained

1/4 white onion, peeled, halved lengthwise, and thinly sliced

1 large cucumber, halved lengthwise and thinly sliced

Dressing

¼ cup extra-virgin olive oil

2 tbsp. apple cider vinegar

Coarse salt and black pepper

Combine all of the dressing ingredients.

Toss with the rest of the ingredients and combine well.

Kale Spinach and Zucchini with Cream Cheese Salad

Preparation time: 15 minutes
Cooking time: 0 minutes
Servings: 4

Ingredients:

1 bunch Kale, rinsed and drained

1 bunch Spinach, rinsed and drained

1/4 white onion, peeled, halved lengthwise, and thinly sliced

1 large Zucchini halved lengthwise ,thinly sliced and blanched

5 ounces cream cheese

Dressing

¼ cup extra-virgin olive oil

2 splashes white wine vinegar

Coarse salt and black pepper

Combine all of the dressing ingredients.

Toss with the rest of the ingredients and combine well.

Artichoke Spinach and Enoki Mushroom Salad

Preparation time: 15 minutes
Cooking time: 0 minutes
Servings: 4

Ingredients:

1 Artichoke, rinsed and drained

1 bunch Spinach, rinsed and drained

15 Enoki Mushrooms, thinly sliced

1/4 white onion, peeled, halved lengthwise, and thinly sliced

1 large cucumber, halved lengthwise and thinly sliced

5 ounces feta cheese, crumbled

Dressing

¼ cup extra-virgin olive oil

2 splashes white wine vinegar

Coarse salt and black pepper

Combine all of the dressing ingredients.

Toss with the rest of the ingredients and combine well.

Kale and Artichoke Salad

Preparation time: 15 minutes
Cooking time: 0 minutes
Servings: 4

Ingredients:

1 bunch Kale, rinsed and drained

1 Artichoke, rinsed and drained

1 large cucumber, halved lengthwise and thinly sliced

5 ounces mozarella cheese, shredded

Dressing

¼ cup extra-virgin olive oil

2 splashes white wine vinegar

Coarse salt and black pepper

Combine all of the dressing ingredients.

Toss with the rest of the ingredients and combine well.

Kale and Romaine Lettuce Salad

Preparation time: 15 minutes
Cooking time: 0 minutes
Servings: 4

Ingredients:

1 bunch Kale, rinsed and drained

1 bunch Romaine Lettuce, rinsed and drained

1/4 white onion, peeled, halved lengthwise, and thinly sliced

1 large cucumber, halved lengthwise and thinly sliced

5 ounces cream cheese, crumbled

Dressing

¼ cup extra-virgin olive oil

2 tbsp. apple cider vinegar

Coarse salt and black pepper

Combine all of the dressing ingredients.

Toss with the rest of the ingredients and combine well.

Mixed Green and Gouda Cheese Salad

Preparation time: 15 minutes
Cooking time: 0 minutes
Servings: 4

Ingredients:

1 bunch Meslcun, rinsed and drained

1 bunch Boston Lettuce, rinsed and drained

10 Tomatillos, halved lengthwise, seeded, and thinly sliced

1/4 white onion, peeled, halved lengthwise, and thinly sliced

1 large Zucchini halved lengthwise ,thinly sliced and blanched

5 ounces gouda cheese, shredded

Dressing

¼ cup extra-virgin olive oil

2 splashes white wine vinegar

Coarse salt and black pepper

Combine all of the dressing ingredients.

Toss with the rest of the ingredients and combine well.

Iceberg Lettuce and Endive Salad
Preparation time: 15 minutes
Cooking time: 0 minutes
Servings: 4

Ingredients:

1 bunch Iceberg Lettuce, rinsed and drained

1 bunch Endive, rinsed and drained

1/4 white onion, peeled, halved lengthwise, and thinly sliced

1 large cucumber, halved lengthwise and thinly sliced

Dressing

¼ cup extra-virgin olive oil

2 splashes white wine vinegar

Coarse salt and black pepper

Combine all of the dressing ingredients.

Toss with the rest of the ingredients and combine well.

Artichoke and Spinach Salad

Preparation time: 15 minutes
Cooking time: 0 minutes
Servings: 4

Ingredients:

1 Artichoke, rinsed and drained

1 bunch Spinach, rinsed and drained

3 Heirloom tomatoes, halved lengthwise, seeded, and thinly sliced

1/4 white onion, peeled, halved lengthwise, and thinly sliced

1 large cucumber, halved lengthwise and thinly sliced

5 ounces ricotta cheese

Dressing

¼ cup extra-virgin olive oil

2 splashes white wine vinegar

Coarse salt and black pepper

Combine all of the dressing ingredients.

Toss with the rest of the ingredients and combine well.

Kale and Spinach with Parmesan Cheese Salad

Preparation time: 15 minutes
Cooking time: 0 minutes
Servings: 4

Ingredients:

1 bunch Kale, rinsed and drained

1 bunch Spinach, rinsed and drained

15 Enoki Mushrooms, thinly sliced

1/4 white onion, peeled, halved lengthwise, and thinly sliced

1 large cucumber, halved lengthwise and thinly sliced

5 ounces parmesan cheese, shredded

Dressing

¼ cup extra-virgin olive oil

2 splashes white wine vinegar

Coarse salt and black pepper

Combine all of the dressing ingredients.

Toss with the rest of the ingredients and combine well.

Carrots and Plum Tomato with Cream Cheese Salad

Preparation time: 15 minutes
Cooking time: 0 minutes
Servings: 4

Ingredients:

1 cup baby carrots, chopped

1/4 white onion, peeled, halved lengthwise, and thinly sliced

1 large cucumber, halved lengthwise and thinly sliced

5 ounces cream cheese, crumbled

Dressing

¼ cup extra-virgin olive oil

2 tbsp. apple cider vinegar

Coarse salt and black pepper

Combine all of the dressing ingredients.

Toss with the rest of the ingredients and combine well.

Corn and Plum Tomato with Cottage Cheese Salad

Preparation time: 15 minutes
Cooking time: 0 minutes
Servings: 4

Ingredients:

1 cup baby corn (canned), drained

1/4 white onion, peeled, halved lengthwise, and thinly sliced

1 large Zucchini halved lengthwise, thinly sliced and blanched

5 ounces cottage cheese, crumbled

Dressing

¼ cup extra-virgin olive oil

2 splashes white wine vinegar

Coarse salt and black pepper

Combine all of the dressing ingredients.

Toss with the rest of the ingredients and combine well.

Boston Lettuce and Baby Corn Salad

Preparation time: 15 minutes
Cooking time: 0 minutes
Servings: 4

Ingredients:

1 bunch Boston Lettuce, rinsed and drained

1 cup baby corn (canned), drained

1 large cucumber, halved lengthwise and thinly sliced

5 ounces monterey jack cheese, shredded

Dressing

¼ cup extra-virgin olive oil

2 splashes white wine vinegar

Coarse salt and black pepper

Combine all of the dressing ingredients.

Toss with the rest of the ingredients and combine well.

Baby Corn and Endive Salad

Preparation time: 15 minutes
Cooking time: 0 minutes
Servings: 4

Ingredients:

1 cup baby corn (canned), drained

1 bunch Endive, rinsed and drained

1/4 white onion, peeled, halved lengthwise, and thinly sliced

1 large Zucchini halved lengthwise ,thinly sliced and blanched

5 ounces pecorino romano cheese, shredded

Dressing

¼ cup extra-virgin olive oil

2 tbsp. apple cider vinegar

Coarse salt and black pepper

Combine all of the dressing ingredients.

Toss with the rest of the ingredients and combine well.

Broccoli and Tomatillo Salad

Preparation time: 15 minutes
Cooking time: 0 minutes
Servings: 4

Ingredients:

9 broccoli florets, blanched and drained

10 Tomatillos, halved lengthwise, seeded, and thinly sliced

1/4 white onion, peeled, halved lengthwise, and thinly sliced

1 large cucumber, halved lengthwise and thinly sliced

5 ounces gouda cheese, shredded

Dressing

¼ cup extra-virgin olive oil

2 splashes white wine vinegar

Coarse salt and black pepper

Combine all of the dressing ingredients.

Toss with the rest of the ingredients and combine well.

Kale and Cauliflower Salad

Preparation time: 15 minutes
Cooking time: 0 minutes
Servings: 4

Ingredients:

1 bunch Kale, rinsed and drained

9 cauliflower florets, blanched and drained

1 large Zucchini halved lengthwise ,thinly sliced and blanched

5 ounces pepperjack cheese, shredded

Dressing

¼ cup extra-virgin olive oil

2 splashes white wine vinegar

Coarse salt and black pepper

Combine all of the dressing ingredients.

Toss with the rest of the ingredients and combine well.

Spinach and Broccoli Salad

Preparation time: 15 minutes
Cooking time: 0 minutes
Servings: 4

Ingredients:

1 bunch Spinach, rinsed and drained

8 broccoli florets, blanched and drained

1 large cucumber, halved lengthwise and thinly sliced

5 ounces ricotta cheese

Dressing

¼ cup extra-virgin olive oil

2 splashes white wine vinegar

Coarse salt and black pepper

Combine all of the dressing ingredients.

Toss with the rest of the ingredients and combine well.

Endives Spinach & Broccoli Salad

Preparation time: 15 minutes
Cooking time: 0 minutes
Servings: 4

Ingredients:

1 bunch Endives, rinsed and drained

8 broccoli florets, blanched and drained

1 bunch Spinach, rinsed and drained

5 ounces cottage cheese, crumbled

Dressing

¼ cup extra-virgin olive oil

2 splashes white wine vinegar

Coarse salt and black pepper

Combine all of the dressing ingredients.

Toss with the rest of the ingredients and combine well.

Artichoke Kale and Broccoli Salad

Preparation time: 15 minutes
Cooking time: 0 minutes
Servings: 4

Ingredients:

1 Artichoke, rinsed and drained

1 bunch Kale, rinsed and drained

8 broccoli florets, blanched and drained

5 ounces mozarella cheese, shredded

1 ounce blue cheese, crumbled

Dressing

¼ cup extra-virgin olive oil

2 splashes white wine vinegar

Coarse salt and black pepper

Combine all of the dressing ingredients.

Toss with the rest of the ingredients and combine well.

Baby Corn and Endive Salad

Preparation time: 15 minutes
Cooking time: 0 minutes
Servings: 4

Ingredients:

1 cup baby corn (canned), drained

1 bunch Collard Greens, rinsed and drained

1 Artichoke, rinsed and drained

5 ounces pecorino romano cheese, shredded

1 ounces cream cheese, crumbled

Dressing

¼ cup extra-virgin olive oil

2 tbsp. apple cider vinegar

Coarse salt and black pepper

Combine all of the dressing ingredients.

Toss with the rest of the ingredients and combine well.

Mixed Green and Baby Carrot Salad

Preparation time: 15 minutes
Cooking time: 0 minutes
Servings: 4

Ingredients:

1 bunch Meslcun, rinsed and drained

1 cup baby carrots, chopped

1 bunch Romaine Lettuce, rinsed and drained

5 ounces monterey jack cheese, shredded

Dressing

¼ cup extra-virgin olive oil

2 splashes white wine vinegar

Coarse salt and black pepper

Combine all of the dressing ingredients.

Toss with the rest of the ingredients and combine well.

Tomatillo and Baby Corn Salad

Preparation time: 15 minutes
Cooking time: 0 minutes
Servings: 4

Ingredients:

10 Tomatillos, halved lengthwise, seeded, and thinly sliced

1 cup baby corn (canned), drained

1 bunch Endive, rinsed and drained

1 Artichoke, rinsed and drained

1 ounces monterey jack cheese, shredded

5 ounces cheddar cheese , shredded

Dressing

¼ cup extra-virgin olive oil

2 splashes white wine vinegar

Coarse salt and black pepper

Combine all of the dressing ingredients.

Toss with the rest of the ingredients and combine well.

Warm Corn Salad

Preparation time: 15 minutes
Cooking time: 10 minutes
Servings: 4

Ingredients

1 teaspoon of butter

2 fresh corn, kernels are cut from the cob

½ diced red onion

1 tablespoon of chopped fresh parsley

pinch of salt to taste

freshly ground black pepper to sprinkle

1 tablespoon of chopped chives

Directions

Take a skillet and melt the butter in it over medium-low heat. Add the fresh corn kernels and chopped red onion. Cook for about 5 minutes till they the red onion gets soft and tender. Mix in the parsley, and season with a pinch of salt and pepper. Garnish with chives and serve.

Enjoy!

Sautéed Mange tout

Preparation time: 15 minutes
Cooking time: 10 minutes
Servings: 4

Ingredient

3 ½ ounces mange tout

1 teaspoon toasted sesame seeds

1 tablespoon soy sauce

3 tablespoons of extra virgin olive oil

Slices of garlic (optional)

Salt and pepper to taste

Directions

Wash the mange touts and remove the strings. Add them to a microwave safe bowl. Add the soy sauce, garlic (optional) and olive oil and cover the bowl completely, making it air tight. Microwave it till they become crisp and tender (this takes about 3 – 5 minutes). Transfer to a serving dish. Sprinkle some toasted sesame seeds, salt and pepper and this quick and easy dish is ready to serve.

Enjoy!

Roasted Cauliflower with Parmesan

Preparation time: 5 minutes
Cooking time: 20 minutes
Servings: 4

Ingredients

1 large cauliflower, cut into florets

4 tablespoons of extra virgin olive oil

1 cup grated Parmesan cheese

Salt to taste

Freshly ground black pepper to taste

2½ tablespoons of minced garlic

Directions

Preheat the oven to 400 degrees F. Take a casserole dish and grease it well with some cooking spray. Take a re-sealable bag and add the olive oil, minced garlic and cauliflower florets to it and shake it well, until the olive oil coats the florets completely. Pour the contents of the re-sealable bag into the greased casserole dish. Sprinkle salt and pepper for seasoning. Bake in the preheated oven for 20-25 minutes. Add the grated Parmesan cheese to the cauliflower florets and broil it for a few more minutes. Cook until the cauliflower gets a hint of brown color to it. Serve hot.

Enjoy!

Buttery Spinach

Preparation time: 5 minutes
Cooking time: 20 minutes
Servings: 4

Ingredients

2 packets of spinach (frozen)

½ cup butter

Salt to taste

Pinch of garlic powder to taste

Directions

Take the packaged frozen spinach in a bowl. Rinse it well with cold water for several minutes. Then allow it to drain completely. Once drained, cut into long strips. Heat a sauce pan over medium-low heat. Add the butter and then the chopped spinach. Add a bit more butter if you wish to have a more buttery flavor. Cook till the spinach starts to wilt around the edges. Remove onto a serving plate and sprinkle the garlic powder and salt to taste, just before serving. Serve it immediately.

Enjoy!

Parmesan Asparagus

Preparation time: 5 minutes
Cooking time: 20 minutes
Servings: 4

Ingredients

1 pound asparagus spears

1 cup shredded Parmesan cheese

Freshly ground black pepper to season

1½ tablespoons of extra virgin olive oil

1 teaspoon Balsamic Vinegar

Directions

Firstly, preheat the oven to 400 degrees F. Wash the asparagus thoroughly and arrange on a baking sheet. Drizzle the olive oil and toss well until the olive oil uniformly coats the asparagus. Top the asparagus with the shredded Parmesan cheese. Sprinkle some black pepper. Now, pop the baking sheet into the preheated oven and bake for about 15 minutes. When the asparagus turns crisp and tender and cheese has completely melted, remove from the baking sheet on to a serving plate. Sprinkle the Balsamic vinegar and serve hot.

Enjoy!

Roasted Brussels sprouts

Preparation time: 5 minutes
Cooking time: 20 minutes
Servings: 4

Ingredients

2 pounds of Brussels sprouts, ends are trimmed and yellow leaves discarded

3 tablespoons of extra virgin olive oil

A pinch of salt to taste

Sprinkle freshly ground black pepper for taste

Directions

Firstly, preheat the oven to 400 degrees F. Wash the sprouts thoroughly. In a re-sealable bag, add the Brussels sprouts, olive oil and a pinch of salt and freshly ground black pepper in it. Seal the bag and shake well until the olive oil coats the sprouts. Spread the Brussels sprouts on a greased baking tray in a single layer and pop into the preheated oven. Bake for about 35 to 40 minutes, continuously turning the Brussels sprouts at an interval of 6 minutes. Keep a check of the heat, so that they don't burn up. When the Brussels sprouts get a dark brown to blackish hue know that they are ready to serve. Taste and season accordingly. Serve immediately.

Enjoy!

Honey Roasted Red Potatoes
Preparation time: 5 minutes
Cooking time: 20 minutes
Servings: 4

Ingredients

A pound of quartered red potatoes

One finely diced onion

2 tablespoons of melted butter

1 tablespoon of honey

A teaspoon of dry mustard

a pinch salt to taste

1 pinch of freshly ground black pepper

Directions

Firstly, preheat the oven to 325 degrees F. Coat a baking dish with nonstick cooking spray. Arrange potatoes in a single layer on the prepared baking dish, and top them with the onion. In a bowl, mix melted butter, honey, mustard, pinch of salt and pepper. Brush this mix on the potatoes and onion. Bake till the potatoes are tender. Serve hot.

Enjoy!

Fried Kale

Preparation time: 5 minutes
Cooking time: 20 minutes
Servings: 4

Ingredients

A bunch of kale

4-5 minced garlic cloves

Generous drizzle of olive oil

Pinch of salt and pepper to taste

Directions

Take fresh kale leaves and wash well. Remove the stems and tear the leaves into bite sized pieces. Heat a pot over medium-high heat and drizzle some olive oil in it. Add the minced garlic into the oil and cook until the garlic is soft. Add the pieces of kale leaves and continue to stir until the leaves start to wilt. It takes about 5 to 6 minutes for leaves to turn into bright green. Serve immediately.

Enjoy!

Asparagus with Balsamic Butter Sauce

Preparation time: 5 minutes
Cooking time: 20 minutes
Servings: 4

Ingredients

A bunch of trimmed fresh asparagus

Cooking spray to grease

Pinch of salt

Pepper to taste

2 tablespoons butter

1 tablespoon of soy sauce

Little drizzle of balsamic vinegar

Directions

Firstly, preheat the oven to 400 degrees F. Wash the asparagus and arrange the asparagus on a baking sheet. Spray with cooking spray. Season with salt and pepper. Bake for about 12 minutes in the preheated oven till the asparagus are tender. Melt about 2 tablespoons of butter over medium heat or put in a microwave safe bowl and microwave for about 30 seconds. Once the butter is liquefied stir in a drizzle of soy sauce and balsamic vinegar. Pour this over the baked asparagus and serve immediately.

Enjoy!

Parmesan Cauliflower

Preparation time: 5 minutes
Cooking time: 20 minutes
Servings: 4

Ingredients

1 whole fresh Cauliflower

1 stick of butter

1½ tablespoons of Mayonnaise

1 teaspoon of mustard (prepared)

1 cup grated parmesan cheese

Oregano to taste

Directions

Firstly, steam the whole cauliflower and place it on a pie plate. Take a mixing bowl and mix Mayonnaise and the prepared mustard. Spread this mixture on the steamed cauliflower. Top it up with the grated Parmesan cheese. Pop it into an oven which was preheated to 400 degrees F. Bake for about 30 minutes, till the cheese melts and top with a pinch of oregano and serve immediately.

Enjoy!

Candied Carrots

Preparation time: 5 minutes
Cooking time: 20 minutes
Servings: 4

Ingredients

5 ounces fresh carrots, cut into 2 inch pieces

2 tablespoons of diced butter

1 tablespoon packed brown sugar

1 pinch of salt to taste

1 pinch of freshly ground black pepper

Directions

Boil the carrots in a pot of salted water. Reduce heat and let it simmer. Cook for about 25 to 35 minutes. Do not overcook the carrots; they should be tender, yet firm. Drain the carrots. Reduce the heat to its lowest and return the carrots to the pan. Now, stir in diced butter, brown sugar, pinch of salt and pepper. Cook for about 4 to 6 minutes, until they get caramelized. Serve them hot.

Enjoy!

Grilled Vegetables

Preparation time: 5 minutes
Cooking time: 20 minutes
Servings: 4

Ingredients

1 cup summer squash, cut into juliennes

1 cup fresh zucchini, cut into juliennes

1 cup florets of cauliflower

1 cup asparagus spears

1cup bell peppers, diced

1 cup onions. diced

Extra virgin olive oil

Pinch of salt

Pepper to taste

Directions

Take all the fresh vegetables and wash them thoroughly with cold water before chopping them. Preheat the oven grill. Place the vegetables in a large mixing bowl. Drizzle some olive oil, pinch of salt and pepper. Toss gently so that the vegetables get uniformly coated. Now arrange them on grill sprayed with some cooking spray. Grill them for about half an minute till they are tender.

Enjoy!

Broccoli in Butter sauce

Preparation time: 5 minutes
Cooking time: 20 minutes
Servings: 4

Ingredients

A Fresh Broccoli, cut into florets

3 tablespoons butter

3 Minced garlic cloves

3 tablespoons of lime juice

Salt to taste

Pinch of pepper

Directions

Firstly, steam the broccoli. Boil it till it is tender and drain. Melt the butter in a saucepan over a medium heat and sauté minced garlic. Now, remove the saucepan from the heat and add the lemon juice. Stir well. Then pour this mixture onto the steamed broccoli. Sprinkle some salt and black pepper to taste. Serve this delicious dish hot within 15-20 minutes of preparing it for maximum taste.

Enjoy!

Honeyed peanuts

Preparation time: 5 minutes
Cooking time: 20 minutes
Servings: 4

Ingredients

1 cup peanuts

Drizzle of Canola oil

5 tablespoons Honey

Pinch of cinnamon

Directions

Take a skillet and heat it over medium heat and grease it with canola oil. Now, add the peanuts to the skillet and keep them stirring them around till they get toasted and a nutty aroma fills the kitchen. Sprinkle cinnamon and honey to the pan. Continue cooking for about 3 to 4 minutes till the honey becomes sticky and starts caramelizing. Remove from heat and place the peanuts on wax paper and let them cool a bit. Break apart and cool. Serve warm and store the leftover peanuts in an air tight container away from direct sunlight.

Enjoy!

Microwave Potato Chips

Preparation time: 5 minutes
Cooking time: 10 minutes
Servings: 4

Ingredients

4-5 potatoes (large)

Garlic powder to taste

Cayenne pepper to taste

Dried dill weed to taste

Salt for seasoning

Oil (Vegetable oil is preferred)

Directions

Take the potatoes, wash them well and peel the skin. Cut them in thin slices. Place the potato slices in a bowl, along with salt and cover with water and let them sit for about 10-12 minutes. Drain and arrange the potato slices on a microwave safe tray, which has already been greased with some vegetable oil. Now sprinkle Cayenne pepper, garlic powder and dried dill weed. Sprinkle a bit of oil over the potato chips and microwave for 5-6 minutes.

Enjoy!

Baked Eggplant

Preparation time: 5 minutes
Cooking time: 15 minutes
Servings: 4

Ingredients

1 large eggplant

1/3rd cup of Mayonnaise

1 cup breadcrumbs

½ cup of grated Parmesan

1 large onion, minced

Dried Italian seasoning to sprinkle

Cooking spray

Directions

Preheat the oven to 400 degrees F. Wash and cut the eggplant into ½ inch thick slices. Arrange these slices on a baking sheet which has been sprayed with cooking spray. In a separate bowl, mix together the mayonnaise and minced onion and spread them over the sliced eggplants. In another bowl, mix breadcrumbs, Parmesan and Italian seasoning and drown the eggplants in this mixture and put them back to the sheet. Bake in the preheated oven for about 10-12 minutes or until the eggplant is firm yet tender to touch. Serve hot.

Enjoy!

Spinach strawberry salad
Preparation time: 5 minutes
Cooking time: 20 minutes
Servings: 4

Ingredients

1 packet fresh spinach, torn apart into bite sized pieces

1 packet fresh strawberries, cut into quarters

Toasted pecans

1 cup Red wine vinegar, raspberry flavor

½ cup sugar

1 teaspoon dry mustard

Drizzle of vegetable oil

2 teaspoons of poppy seeds

Directions

Take a bowl and combine red wine raspberry vinegar, sugar, dried mustard, poppy seeds and drizzle of vegetable oil. Mix them well and your dressing is ready. Now, take a big salad mixing bowl and add the fresh spinach. Drizzle the dressing and start tossing, in order to ensure uniform coating. Add the fresh strawberries to the bowl. Top with some chopped toasted pecans. Serve the salad immediately.

Enjoy!

Carrot Quinoa Burgers

Preparation time: 5 minutes
Cooking time: 10 minutes
Servings: 4

Ingredients:

2 carrots, peeled and grated

1 parsnip, peeled and grated

1 1/2 cups cooked quinoa

1 cup canned white beans

2 tablespoons rice flour

Salt, pepper (to taste)

Directions:

In a food processor, pulse the beans until a paste forms. Put paste into large mixing bowl and add remaining ingredient list.

Wet your hands and mold mixture into a burger shape.

Add one tablespoon of olive oil to a frying pan on medium heat. Burger will need to be cooked 5–6 minutes on each side, until golden brown.

Serve on your vegan roll, using toppings of your choice and tastiest condiments.

Spicy Chickpea Oat Burgers

Preparation time: 5 minutes
Cooking time: 20 minutes
Servings: 4

Ingredients:

1/4 cup rolled oats

3 cups canned chickpeas, drained

2 garlic cloves

1 teaspoon curry powder

2 tablespoons chopped coriander

3 tablespoons olive oil

Salt, pepper (to taste)

Directions:

In a food processor, pulse chickpeas and oats until smooth. Add to the processor, garlic cloves, curry and coriander. Pulse to combine and add mixture to a medium mixing bowl, salt and pepper.

Wet your hands and mold mixture into a burger shape.

Add one tablespoon of olive oil to a frying pan on medium heat. Burger will need to be cooked 5-6 minutes on each side, until golden brown and crispy. If greasy, dab with paper towels to dry.

Serve on your vegan roll, using toppings of your choice and favorite condiments.

Cashew with Lentil Burgers

Preparation time: 5 minutes
Cooking time: 10 minutes
Servings: 4

Ingredients:

1 3/4 cups canned chickpeas, rinsed and drained

2 1/2 cups canned lentils, rinsed and drained

1/2 cup cashew pieces

2 carrots, peeled and grated

3 garlic cloves, minced

1 green onion, chopped

2 tablespoon olive oil

1 teaspoon curry powder

1 teaspoon turmeric powder

4 tablespoons flour

2 cups breadcrumbs

3 tablespoons olive oil

Salt, pepper (to taste)

Directions:

In a large frying pan, sauté onions and garlic until onion is translucent. Stir in the carrots, and cook until desired tenderness. Place mixture in a large mixing bowl and combine with lentils, curry powder, and turmeric.

Put the chickpeas and cashew nuts in a food processor and pulse a few times until a smooth paste forms. Combine paste with the vegetable mix then add the flour and salt/pepper. Coat burgers with breadcrumbs.

Wet your hands and mold mixture into a burger shape.

Add one tablespoon of olive oil to a frying pan on medium heat. Burger will need to be cooked 5–6 minutes on each side, until golden brown and crispy. If greasy, dab with paper towels to dry.

Serve on your vegan roll, using toppings of your choice and favorite condiments.

Spicy Quinoa Burgers

Preparation time: 5 minutes
Cooking time: 20 minutes
Servings: 4

Ingredients:

1 small onion, chopped

1 green pepper, deseeded and chopped

2 garlic cloves, minced

1 cup canned black beans

1 cup cooked quinoa

1 teaspoon taco seasoning

2 tablespoons flax seeds

1/2 cup breadcrumbs

2 tablespoons all purpose flour

Salt, pepper (to taste)

Directions:

Add 6 tablespoons of water to flax seed in small mixing bowl and let soak.

Sauté onions and garlic in medium frying pan with one tablespoon of olive oil for approximately 4 minutes, until onions are translucent. Allow to cool and put in a large mixing bowl.

In a food processor, pulse half of the quinoa and all of the beans until smooth. Place mixture in large mixing bowl with the onions and garlic, and add remaining quinoa, taco seasoning and green pepper. Combine well and add flour, breadcrumbs, and flax seed mixture.

Wet your hands and mold mixture into a burger shape.

Add one tablespoon of olive oil to a frying pan on medium heat. Burger will need to be cooked 5–6 minutes on each side, until golden brown and crispy.

Peanut Butter Burgers

Preparation time: 5 minutes
Cooking time: 20 minutes
Servings: 4

Ingredients:

2 cups canned chickpeas

3 tablespoons peanut butter

1 teaspoon lemon juice

1 teaspoon soy sauce

1 teaspoon fresh grated ginger

1 green onion, chopped

1/4 teaspoon chili flakes

3 tablespoons coconut oil

Salt, pepper (to taste)

Directions:

Grind the chickpeas in a food processor or blender. Add peanut butter, soy sauce, lemon juice and ginger to food processor and create a smooth paste on pulse setting. Put paste mixture in a large mixing bowl and combine with green onion, chili flakes, and salt/pepper.

Wet your hands and mold mixture into a burger shape. Add coconut oil to a frying pan on medium heat. Burger will need to be cooked 5–6 minutes on each side, until golden brown and crispy around the edges.

Chapter 5: Dinner

Glazed Carrots

Preparation time: 5 minutes
Cooking time: 10 minutes
Servings: 4

Ingredients

1 pound fresh carrots

1 and a half stick of butter

Sugar to taste

Salt to taste

6-7 tablespoons of maple syrup

3 tablespoons brown sugar

Chopped fresh parsley

Directions

Heat a large pot with water in it. Cut the carrots into slices horizontally and add them to the pot along with about half stick of the butter, sugar and salt. Boil and then simmer till the carrots become tender. Drain and keep aside. Heat a skillet over medium heat melt rest of the butter in it. Add the maple syrup and brown sugar to it. Keep on stirring till the sugar dissolves. Add the carrots and cook for another 5-6 minutes. Sprinkle salt, pepper and chopped parsley over it.

Enjoy!

Homemade Cranberry sauce

Preparation time: 10 minutes
Cooking time: 15 minutes
Servings: 5

Ingredients

12 ounces of fresh juicy cranberries

1 cup sugar or artificial sweetener

1 cup orange juice (you may use 1 cup of plain water)

Directions

Take a big bowl, fill it with water and rinse the fresh cranberries very well. Drain. Add 1 cup of sugar or artificial sweetener and 1 cup of water or orange juice to the cranberries. Mix them thoroughly and transfer them to a saucepan and bring the mix to a boil. Once bubbling, reduce the heat and simmer for a while. Remove from the heat when the sauce is thick and cool to room temperature. Pour the sauce into an airtight container and chill in the refrigerator for at least 8 minutes before serving.

Enjoy!

Spicy Onion Rings
Preparation time: 10 minutes
Cooking time: 15 minutes
Servings: 5

Ingredients

1 cup flour

Warm or cold water, as needed

Salt to taste

Paprika to make it spicy, to taste

4 large onions

Vegetable or extra virgin olive oil, for frying

Directions

Firstly, take 1 cup of flour (self-rising) and mix it with warm or cold water until you attain a uniformly runny consistency. Now, add paprika to make it spicy and salt according to your taste.

Cut the fresh onions into rings and drench the rings into the mixture until evenly coated. Now, deep fry the onion rings till they become crispy and crunchy. Serve them hot and delicious.

Enjoy!

Cheesy Dip rice

Preparation time: 10 minutes
Cooking time: 15 minutes
Servings: 5

Ingredients

A handful of salad rocket

1 cup rice

Extra virgin olive oil

1 container tortilla cheese dip

Water, as needed

Hot vegetable stock, as needed

Salt and pepper to taste

Oregano (if you wish)

Directions

First, steam the rice in a mixture of the water and vegetable stock (mixed in a 1:1 ratio). Drain it. Add drizzle of extra virgin olive oil, tortilla cheese dip to the cooked rice and mix them thoroughly. Add a handful of salad rocket. Again mix thoroughly. You can serve this dish steaming hot. You may refrigerate this prepared dish and serve it cold. The dish tastes best when it is served cold.

Enjoy!

Baked Butternut Squash Fries

Preparation time: 10 minutes
Cooking time: 10 minutes
Servings: 5

Ingredients

1 fresh butternut squash

Drizzle of extra virgin olive oil

Garlic salt to season

Freshly ground black pepper to taste

Directions

Wash the butternut squash, peel off the skin and cut it into ½ inch slices. Then preheat the oven to 400 degrees F. Arrange the butternut squash slices in a single layer in a greased baking tray. Drizzle extra virgin olive oil and season with a pinch of garlic salt and freshly ground black pepper. Pop into the preheated oven and bake till they are crispy and crunchy. Serve the fries hot with sprinkle of salt.

Enjoy!

Vegetable cous cous

Preparation time: 10 minutes
Cooking time: 10 minutes
Servings: 5

Ingredients

1 cup Couscous

½ cup mushrooms (any type)

½ cup peeled tomatoes, diced

½ cup sweet corn kernels

1/2 cup chickpeas

Salt to taste

Black pepper to taste

Directions

Fill a pot with water and add the couscous and bring it to a boil. When the couscous is cooked, drain the water. The cooking process should take about 5 to 6 minutes. Meanwhile, chop the mushrooms and place in a microwaveable bowl. Then add the tomatoes, chickpeas and the sweet corn to the mushrooms. Place this in the microwave for about 2 to 3 minutes. Now add this to the cooked couscous. Mix well and season with salt and pepper. Serve hot.

Enjoy!

Bread Pizza
Preparation time: 10 minutes
Cooking time: 20 minutes
Servings: 5

Ingredients

12 bread slices

½ cup tomato sauce

4 tablespoons melted butter

½ cup mozzarella cheese, grated

2 onions

2 tomatoes

2 capsicums

2 tablespoons of olive oil

A pinch of oregano

Salt and pepper to taste

Directions

M Wash the onions, tomatoes and capsicums and dice uniformly. Put them in a bowl and add the olive oil, pinch of oregano, salt and pepper and mix well. Place the bowl in the freezer for about 5 minutes. You can store this mix in the fridge for at least 3 days. Pour the tomato sauce in a bowl and mix in the butter. Spread it on slice of bread. Spread a layer of the mozzarella, then the vegetable mix and top it with the mozzarella and heat in the microwave till the cheese melts. Serve immediately.

Enjoy

Peanut Rice
Preparation time: 10 minutes
Cooking time: 15 minutes
Servings: 5

Ingredients

7-8 cups of rice

2 large onions, finely chopped

1 cup soy sauce

2 ½ tubs of creamy peanut butter

1 garlic clove, finely chopped

4 chilies

Salt to taste

Pepper to taste

Directions

Take a pot with water and add the rice to. Bring it to boil and simmer until the rice is cooked. Keep aside. Take a skillet and stir fry the garlic, chilies and onions until soft. Pour the soy sauce and peanut butter to the rice and mix well. Add the contents in the skillet into the rice and peanut butter mix and heat on a low heat for 6-12 minutes, continuously stirring it. Serve hot.

Enjoy!

Delightful Beans

Preparation time: 5 minutes
Cooking time: 25 minutes
Servings: 5

Ingredients

1 can of beans (preferably soya beans)

1 clove of garlic, finely chopped

2 tomatoes, peeled and chopped

1 cube of vegetable stock

1 fresh onion, chopped

Drizzle of Vegetable oil

Directions

Drizzle a bit of vegetable oil in a medium sized skillet over medium heat. Add the onions and garlic to the skillet and sauté until tender. Fill a pot with some water and heat until gently simmering. Add in the vegetable stock cube and mix well. Pour the stock into the skillet with the onions and garlic and add the tomatoes and beans to it. Cook on a medium flame, for about 10 minutes or until the beans are tender. Serve hot.

Enjoy!

Fried Onion and Cabbage

Preparation time: 10 minutes
Cooking time: 15 minutes
Servings: 5

Ingredients

1 large potato

1 large red onion

1 head of cabbage

Salt to taste

Freshly ground black pepper to taste

Extra virgin olive oil for sautéing

Directions

Firstly, steam the cabbage and keep it aside. Now, finely dice the onion and fry in a sauce pan with some extra virgin olive oil. Finely grate the potato. As the chopped onion begins to turn brown, add the grated potato to it and mix well. Add the cooked cabbage to the onions and potatoes and mix well .Sprinkle some black pepper and salt according to your taste and serve them hot and crispy.

Enjoy!

Spinach Sauté

Preparation time: 10 minutes
Cooking time: 10 minutes
Servings: 5

Ingredients

2 tablespoons of butter

2 garlic cloves, finely chopped

10 ounce of spinach (fresh)

Pinch of salt

Sprinkle freshly ground black pepper

Juice of 1/2 lemon

Directions

Melt the butter in a sauce pan over medium heat. Add the garlic and stir till it turns is golden brown. Be careful so that the garlic does not burn. Turn to high and add the fresh spinach, flipping every minute, till they start to wilt around the edges. Take the sauce pan off the heat. Season with salt and pepper and add in the lemon juice. Toss well and serve immediately.

Enjoy!

Pumpkin Pancakes

Preparation time: 10 minutes
Cooking time: 15 minutes
Servings: 5

Ingredients

2 cups of coconut flour

1 teaspoon baking powder

A pinch of salt

A pinch of cinnamon

1 cup coconut milk

4 tablespoons melted butter

4 tablespoons maple syrup

Few drops of vanilla extract

Pinch of pie spice

1 cup pumpkin puree

Directions

Mix the flour, baking powder, pinch of salt, cinnamon and pie spice in a bowl and whisk together. In another bowl combine the coconut milk, pumpkin puree, butter, vanilla extract and maple syrup. Pour this mixture into the dry ingredients and fold in a clockwise motion. Melt some butter on a griddle and pour this batter onto the griddle in circular motions. Cook on both sides until evenly browned.

Enjoy!

Toasted Quinoa Tabbouleh

Preparation time: 10 minutes
Cooking time: 15 minutes
Servings: 5

Ingredients

1 ½ cups of quinoa

1 ¾ teaspoon sea salt, divided

1/3 cup of olive oil

¾ cup lemon juice

2 cloves of garlic

½ teaspoon of ground black pepper

2 cups diced tomatoes

1½cups parsley

3 unpeeled Persian cucumbers

1 cup green onions

½ cup mint leaves

Directions

Rinse quinoa in a strainer under water. Add to a large skillet and heat till golden and fragrant, stirring constantly. Bring water to boil in a saucepan. Add salt (1/4 teaspoons) and then quinoa. Reduce heat and boil again and then simmer for 20 minutes, till the quinoa is soft and all the liquid has been absorbed. Fluff it using fork and place in a bowl. Let it cool. Whisk lemon juice, oil, pepper and garlic with the remaining salt in a bowl. Stir well with tomatoes, cucumbers, parsley, mint leaves and green onions into quinoa. Pour marinade over it and toss till well-coated. Refrigerate to serve chill.

Enjoy!

Bell Pepper, Olive and Arugula Salsa

Preparation time: 10 minutes
Cooking time: 15 minutes
Servings: 5

Ingredients

1 ½ teaspoons olive oil

1 teaspoons fennel seeds

2 small bell peppers (1 yellow and 1 red)

16 Kalamata olives, quartered

½ cup packed baby arugula, chopped

Directions

Take large nonstick pan and heat oil with fennel seeds added, over medium heat. Stir occasionally. Add bell peppers and sauté for about 4 minutes until peppers begin to get tender. Remove the oil and bell peppers into medium sized bowl and mix olives in it. Let it stand for 2 minutes after seasoning with pepper and salt. Let the flavors infuse properly. Combine with arugula and toss till arugula lightly wilted.

Enjoy!

Sweet-and-Sour Baked Tofu

Preparation time: 10 minutes
Cooking time: 10 minutes
Servings: 5

Ingredients

1½ tablespoons soy sauce

1½ tablespoons lime juice

1 tablespoons red chili sauce

½ tablespoons olive oil

½ teaspoons brown sugar

14oz (6 slices) tofu

2 tablespoons roasted peanuts

2 pcs green onions

1 tablespoons ginger

1½ cups shredded red cabbage

2 pc (4" each) Ciabatta rolls, halved lengthwise

Directions

Preheat oil to 400 degrees F. Grease a baking dish with some cooking spray. Whisk together the sugar, soy sauce, chili sauce, lime juice and oil in a bowl. Add tofu slices and marinate for 10 minutes, flipping twice. Transfer tofu to the baking dish and sprinkle peanuts, onion and ginger over it. Bake until brown. Let it cool. Toss cabbage with left over marinade. Discard excess of bread from rolls' center. Place 3 slices of tofu on bottom half and garnish with cabbage. Close sandwich and store in refrigerator.

Enjoy!

Pineapple, cucumber and avocado salsa
Preparation time: 10 minutes
Cooking time: 15 minutes
Servings: 5

Ingredients:

1⅓ cups cucumber

½ pc pineapple, peeled, diced and cored

1/4 cup green onions, sliced

3-4 teaspoons red jalapeno chili, chopped

8oz avocado, peeled, diced and deseeded

Directions

Stir the pineapple, green onions, cucumber and chili together in a bowl. Squeeze the pineapple slices using garlic press, extracting about ¼ cup of juice. Stir juice into salsa and fold in the avocado. Season with pepper and salt if required and let it set for about 5 minutes before you serve. The recipe makes about 3 cups of the appetizer.

Enjoy!

Black-Eyed Pea Chili

Preparation time: 10 minutes
Cooking time: 10 minutes
Servings: 5

Ingredients

1/2 lb. black-eyed peas

2 tablespoons coconut oil

1 cup onion

1 cup green bell pepper

2 teaspoons garlic cloves

1 can (15 oz.) fire-roasted tomatoes

2 tablespoons tomato puree

1 tablespoon chili powder

1 cup vegetable broth

½ cup green onions

Directions

Soak the black-eyed peas in water for 8 hrs. Rinse well. Put the setting to 'sauté' and preheat rice cooker for 2-3 minutes. Add oil and heat. Add onion and sauté. Combine bell pepper and garlic and sauté again for 4 minutes until softened. Stir in the tomato puree, tomatoes and chili powder. Simmer for few minutes. Adjust setting to 'slow cook' and pour in black-eyed peas and vegetable broth. Cook for 5 minutes till the peas are tender. Add pepper and salt and garnish with green onions.

Enjoy!

Japanese Noodle Soup

Preparation time: 10 minutes
Cooking time: 15 minutes
Servings: 5

Ingredients

6 cloves of garlic

4 pieces of green onions

2 pcs (5inch each) Kombu

7 small coins of ginger

¼ cup Tamari sauce

3 tablespoons Mirin

2 teaspoons Sugar

2 cups Shiitake mushrooms

3 pc carrots

4 cups rice noodles, cooked

2 cups snow peas

4 teaspoons sesame oil

2 teaspoons sesame seeds

Directions

Chop the garlic cloves. Put in cooker. Add white parts of green onions along with ginger and Kombu to cooker. Chop green onions and set aside. Add mirin, tamari, water and sugar to the cooker and cook for 6 minutes. Strain and remove solid parts and return liquid back to cooker. Add carrots and mushrooms and cook for 1 minute until vegetables tender. Split noodles in 4 bowls and top with peas. Pour broth and garnish with sesame oil, onions and seeds.

Enjoy!

Curried Cheese and Peach Panini

Preparation time: 10 minutes
Cooking time: 20 minutes
Servings: 5

Ingredients

2 cups cottage cheese 2cups

1 teaspoon curry powder

½ teaspoon ginger

¼ teaspoon lime zest

1/4 cup celery, chopped

2 tablespoons green onion, chopped

10 oz. sour dough baguette

½ cup mango chutney

1 large peach, sliced

8 tablespoons almonds, sliced

Directions

Stir cheese, ginger, curry powder and lime zest in a bowl. Fold in the onions and celery. Set aside. Divide baguette lengths with one side attached. Discard excess bread for filling space. Spread 2 tablespoons chutney and fill with ½ cheese mixture, 2 tablespoons almonds and 4 peach slices. Use cooking spray for spraying Panini tops and coat skillet with cooking spray and put on medium heat. Add Panini and cook for 3 minutes, placing 2 cans weight on it. Flip Panini once and replace weight and cook for 2 more minutes until almost crisp.

Enjoy!

Baked Potato Pizza

Preparation time: 10 minutes
Cooking time: 10 minutes
Servings: 5

Ingredients

3 tablespoons olive oil

1 gluten-free pizza crust, par-baked

1 garlic clove, minced

1 baked potato, sliced

½ cup raw broccoli florets

2/3 cup cheddar cheese, shredded

1/3 cup sour cream

Chives ¼ cup, chopped

Directions

Preheat oven to 425 degrees F. Grease 2 tablespoons oil over par-baked pizza crust. Put the garlic, broccoli florets and sliced potato as toppings. Drizzle 1 tablespoon olive oil and add sour cream and cheddar cheese in dollops. Bake until cheese bubbling, for around 7 minutes. Remove and then sprinkle chives over it. Serve hot.

Enjoy!

Dark Chocolate and Banana Panini

Preparation time: 10 minutes
Cooking time: 10 minutes
Servings: 5

Ingredients

2 bananas, large in size and sliced

8 slices of sourdough bread or sprouted wheat

4 oz. of dark chocolate, bittersweet and chopped

4 teaspoons of honey

Directions

Place the banana slices on 4 slices of bread. Sprinkle 3 tablespoons of chocolate on each of the slices. Add 1 teaspoons of honey. Now, cover with the remaining pieces of bread. Take Panini maker and preheat. Coat the maker with butter flavored cooking spray. Cook the Panini from both the sides for 3-4 minutes. Allow it to cool for 5 minutes and then serve.

Enjoy!

Mediterranean Veggie Burgers

Preparation time: 10 minutes
Cooking time: 25 minutes
Servings: 5

Ingredients

4 oz. of rigatoni

7 oz. of vegetable broth, low sodium

½ cup of red quinoa

1 ½ teaspoon of olive oil

¾ cup of onion, chopped

9 cloves of garlic, finely chopped

1 ½ cups of white beans, cooked

½ cup of broccoli, steamed

¼ cup and 2 tablespoons of green cabbage, shredded finely

3 tablespoons of red bell pepper, finely chopped

2 tablespoons of tomato sauce

6 Kalama olives, sliced

2 tomatoes, oil-packed and sun dried, drained and chopped finely

2 tablespoons of canola oil

Directions

Boil rigatoni in pot of salted water for 19 minutes or until tender. Drain and keep aside 1 ½ cups tight rigatoni. Boil broth and quinoa in a saucepan. Cook for 13 minutes on low heat. Drain. In a small pan, heat oil on medium flame. Add onion and cook for 1 minute. Now, add garlic and cook for another 1 minute. In a processor, process rigatoni and beans until smooth. Pour the batter into a bowl and add quinoa, broccoli, bell pepper, olives, cabbage, tomatoes, and the onion-garlic mixture and combine. Mash the mixture and make patties and brush them with oil. Heat the grill and brush with oil. Place the patties on the grill and cook for 6-7 minutes. Turn the sides and cook again. Serve hot.

Enjoy!

Blue Cheese Radicchio and Fig Sandwiches

Preparation time: 10 minutes
Cooking time: 15 minutes
Servings: 5

Ingredients

3 oz. of blue cheese, crumbled

3 oz. of cream cheese, reduced-fat

8 slices of whole-grain bread, sprouted

8 teaspoons of butter, melted and trans-fat free

4 tablespoons of jam, fig

1 cup of radicchio, sliced thinly

Directions

Mash both the cheese together in a mixing bowl. Set aside few chunks of blue cheese. Apply butter on the 4 slices of bread. Apply some butter on the baking sheet too. Spread 1 tablespoon jam and ¼ cup of radicchio on each slice of bread. Cover the remaining 4 slices with the cheese mixture and place them on top of the radicchio. Now apply the remaining butter on the top of the slices. Take large skillet and heat it on medium heat. Now, cook both the sides of the sandwiches for 3 to 4 minutes until crisp and brown. Serve hot.

Enjoy!

Homemade Tomato Soup

Preparation time: 10 minutes
Cooking time: 15 minutes
Servings: 5

Ingredients

2 tablespoons of olive oil

1 onion, medium sized , chopped

1 tablespoon of tomato paste

2 cloves of garlic, minced

1 teaspoon of sugar

1 can (12 oz.) tomatoes, diced

1 vegetable cube, optional

2 teaspoons of vinegar, balsamic

½ teaspoon of thyme, dried

Directions

Take a medium sized saucepan and place it on medium heat. Add the chopped onions and sauté for 5 minutes. Add tomato paste, sugar and garlic and cook for 1 minute. Now combine diced tomatoes, vinegar, vegetable cube (if required), thyme and 4 cups of water and bring to a boil. Simmer the soup for 15 minutes. Now remove the saucepan from heat and blend it in a blender. Add pepper and salt if desired. Serve hot.

Enjoy!

Stir-fried Broccoli Florets, stems and Leaves
Preparation time: 10 minutes
Cooking time: 15 minutes
Servings: 5

Ingredients

1 broccoli, large head

1 navel orange, large sized and washed

2 tablespoons of lemon juice

1 tablespoon of soy sauce

1 tablespoon of brown sugar

1 tablespoon of fresh ginger julienned, and 2 teaspoons of minced, divided

1 teaspoon of cornstarch

3 tablespoons of vegetable oil

2 shallots, large sized, peeled and sliced thinly

1 large garlic clove, peeled and sliced thinly

½ teaspoon of salt

Directions

Remove the leaves of broccoli and slice them thinly. Remove the florets and trim them into 1-2 inch florets. Cut the broccoli stalk in thin slices. Peel the zest from orange in about 6-7 long and ½ an inch wide strips. Pile the strips and slice thinly to julienne . Stir 3 tablespoons of orange juice and lemon juice along with soy sauce, minced ginger, brown sugar and cornstarch in a small bowl. Keep aside. Place a wok on medium heat and add broccoli leaves, orange zest julienned, ginger julienned, garlic and shallots. Fry for 2 minutes and remove in a plate. Add the other 1 tablespoon of oil to a wok and heat over medium heat. Add florets and stalks and add salt for seasoning. Combine juice mixture. Allow to cool and then toss with the leaves.

Enjoy!

Tangy Sweet Pizza
Preparation time: 10 minutes
Cooking time: 15 minutes
Servings: 5

Ingredients

¼ cup of tomato pesto, sun-dried

1 Gluten-Free Pizza Crust, par-baked

1 ½ cups of sweet potatoes, cooked and sliced

½ cup of red onion, sliced thinly

2/3 cup of feta cheese, crumbled

2 cups of baby arugula

Directions

Brush the tomato pesto over the Pizza Crust. Add the toppings of red onions, sweet potatoes and feta cheese. Set the oven at 425 degrees F and bake the pizza for 5-7 minutes. Let the cheese melt and toppings turn brown. Remove the pizza from pan and serve after topping the pizza with the baby arugula.

Enjoy!

Fresh Corn and Tomatillo Salsa
Preparation time: 10 minutes
Cooking time: 15 minutes
Servings: 5

Ingredients

1 ½ cups of fresh, husked tomatillos, chopped

1 ½ cups of corn kernels, fresh

6 tablespoons of cilantro, chopped

1 tablespoon of jalapeno chili along with seeds, chopped

1 tablespoon of fresh lime juice

Directions

Take the tomatillos in a small bowl and microwave on high power for 2 minutes till they turn saucy. Scatter the sauce on a pie dish. Shift to freezer for quick cooling. Place a nonstick skillet over medium heat and coat it with cooking spray. Now, add corn and stir for 2 minutes. Allow it to cool and shift to freezer for fast cooling. Now mix jalapeno, lemon juice and cilantro in a bowl. Add corn and tomato sauce to it. Taste and season accordingly.

Enjoy!

Hummus Pie

Preparation time: 10 minutes
Cooking time: 15 minutes
Servings: 5

Ingredients

1 ¼ cups of hummus

1 Gluten Free Pizza Crust, par baked

½ cup of red peppers, roasted and chopped

1/3 cup of red onion, chopped

1 teaspoon of sumac, ground

Cilantro for garnishing

Directions

Spread the hummus over the pizza crust. Add toppings of roasted red peppers, ground sumac and red onion. Bake the pizza in a preheated oven at 425 degrees F for 5-7 minutes. Garnish with the cilantro. Serve hot.

Enjoy!

Red Curry Vegetable Soup

Preparation time: 10 minutes
Cooking time: 20 minutes
Servings: 5

Ingredients

1 tablespoon of canola oil

12 oz. of cauliflower, cut into florets of 1 inch

4 green onions, large sized and sliced thinly, separating the green and white parts

2 tablespoons of Thai red curry paste

4 cups of vegetable broth, low sodium

1 can (15-oz.) of tomatoes, diced and juiced

¾ cup of coconut milk, light

6 oz. of green beans, cut into pieces

1 tablespoon of lime juice

Directions

Put a large saucepan on medium heat and add oil. Add cauliflower and white parts of the green onion and stir for 5 minutes. Stir in the curry paste and mix for 1 more minute. Add the tomatoes and broth with their respective juices. Bring to a boil and simmer for 10 minutes. Combine green beans and coconut milk and simmer for another 5 minutes until tender. Combine lime juice and the rest of the green onions. Serve hot.

Enjoy!

Farmers' Market Pizza

Preparation time: 10 minutes
Cooking time: 15 minutes
Servings: 5

Ingredients

Tomato sauce

1 tablespoon of canola, plus some for oiling grill

3 plum tomatoes

2 tablespoons of oregano, fresh

1 tablespoon of red wine vinegar

1 tablespoon of olive oil

2 garlic cloves, minced

½ teaspoon of salt

½ teaspoon of red pepper flakes

Pizza

1 ½ cups of broccoli florets, large

1 red bell pepper, small and sliced

1 yellow bell pepper, small and sliced

½ red onion, cut into rings

¼ cup of canola oil

1 Par-Baked Pizza Crust

¼ teaspoon of black pepper, ground

Directions

Oil the grill grate and preheat on medium heat. Make tomato sauce by brushing canola oil on the tomatoes. Grill them for 5 minutes. Make the puree of tomatoes, vinegar, garlic, salt, pepper, red chili flakes and oregano in a blender. Shift to bowl. Make pizza by tossing broccoli, onion, bell peppers, canola oil into a bowl. Shift them in grill basket and grill for 5-7 minutes. Slice the bell peppers. Spread tomato sauce on the crust and top with vegetables, grill and cook for 5 more minutes.

Enjoy!

Herbed Macadamia-Almond Cheese

Preparation time: 10 minutes
Cooking time: 10 minutes
Servings: 5

Ingredients

Cheese base

1 cup macadamia nuts

1 cup almonds

½ teaspoon probiotic powder

Add-Ins

¼ cup red onion

1/4 cup parsley

¼ cup pine nuts

2 tablespoons chives

2 tablespoons dill

2 tablespoons lemon juice

1 teaspoon sea salt

¼ teaspoon black pepper

Directions

Soak the macadamia nuts and almonds in water for 8 minute s. Drain and blend with fresh water and probiotic powder until creamy and smooth. Line small colander with wet cheese cloth to extract creamy nut mixture and set the colander to catch liquid in a dish. Fold excess of cloth on the mixture and set aside to ferment. Place 1 can over it after 2 minutes to drain out excess liquid. Transfer the base into bowl and stir in the entire Add-Ins. Store in refrigerator till a week.

Enjoy!

Provencal Tartlets

Preparation time: 10 minutes
Cooking time: 15 minutes
Servings: 5

Ingredients

1 ½ cups green zucchini

1 cup yellow onion

2 ½ cups bell pepper

1 cup fennel bulb

4 ½ teaspoons olive oil

1 ½ teaspoons garlic

1 teaspoon thyme, oregano

1 cup roasted tomatoes

4 tablespoons Gaeta olives

1 tablespoon parsley

2 oz. Asiago cheese

3 tablespoons Parmesan cheese

Masa harina cream cheese dough

Directions

Preheat oven to 400 degrees F. Toss the onion, zucchini, bell pepper and fennel with garlic, oil, oregano and thyme. Arrange vegetables on two baking sheets and roast in the preheated oven for 20 minutes. Transfer in bowl and set aside to cool. Add tomatoes, parsley, olives and cheese to the vegetables and toss. Reduce the oven temperature to 375 degrees. Scoop ¾ cup in each dough center. Fold edges inwardly and chill tarts for 10 minutes. Brush the tarts with some oil. Place on parchment paper. Bake for 30 minutes or until golden.

Enjoy!

Okra and Sweet Potato Fritters

Preparation time: 10 minutes
Cooking time: 15 minutes
Servings: 5

Ingredients

2 ½ cups of okra

1 cup sweet potato

¼ cup shallots

1 tablespoon honey

1 tablespoon soy sauce

½ cup yellow cornmeal

3 tablespoons canola oil

Directions

Combine the sweet potato, okra, honey, shallot, soy sauce and corn meal in a bowl. Refrigerate for about 30 minutes. Wet your hands and divide mixture into 16 golf ball-size spheres and slightly flatten them. Heat the oil on medium heat in a large skillet. Cook fritters for 8 minutes while flipping once. Repeat with remaining oil and spheres. Serve warm fritters with dipping in soy sauce as desired.

Enjoy!

Perfect Roasted Tomatoes

Preparation time: 10 minutes
Cooking time: 15 minutes
Servings: 5

Ingredients

½ teaspoon salt

2 lbs. plum tomatoes, cored and cut into halves crosswise

1 tablespoon olive oil

¼ teaspoon ground pepper

4 sage leaves, chopped

5 thyme sprigs

Directions

Preheat oven to 400 degrees F. Put tomatoes in a baking sheet lined with parchment paper, with its cut-side down. Brush with oil and sprinkle with sage, pepper, salt and thyme. Roast for 45 minutes until the skin blistered and flesh soft. Remove from oven and set aside to cool. Peel off skin and then serve.

Enjoy!

Almond-Cranberry Twist

Preparation time: 10 minutes
Cooking time: 15 minutes
Servings: 5

Ingredients

Filling:

¾ cups toasted almonds

3 tablespoons unsalted butter

¼ cup sugar

1/8 teaspoon salt

2 teaspoons all-purpose flour

½ teaspoon almond extract

1/3 cup dried cranberries

Dough

2 ¼ cups all-purpose flour

3 teaspoons yeast

1/3 cup unsalted butter

1/3 cup sugar

1 ¼ teaspoon salt

2 ¼ cups whole-wheat flour

Directions

Grind half almonds in food processor and add coarsely chopped other halves to it. Beat sugar, butter and salt in blender until smooth. Add flour and almond extract and beat again. Stir well in chopped almonds. Stir flour, yeast and warm water in bowl and prepare dough. Mix butter, salt and sugar into flour-yeast mixture and then add whole-wheat flour. Knead till smooth. Leave for 1 minute to rise. Set dough and make a rectangle on a parchment paper. Spread filling in the center and sprinkle cranberries. Roll as per desired shape and refrigerate. Brush some oil the over braids. Bake in oven until brown and cool.

Enjoy!

The Red-Headed Mary

Preparation time: 10 minutes
Cooking time: 10 minutes
Servings: 5

Ingredients:

4 cups juice of fresh carrots

12 oz. vodka

¼ cup fresh lemon juice

2 tablespoons prepared or fresh horseradish

2 tablespoons vegetarian Worcestershire sauce

Directions

Mix all ingredients and stir well until smooth and consistent in a pitcher. Add seasoning salt and a pinch of ground black pepper for desired taste. Store in a glass mason jar and refrigerate. Chill for around 1 minute and then serve.

Enjoy!

Gluten-Free Pizza Crust

Preparation time: 10 minutes
Cooking time: 15 minutes
Servings: 5

Ingredients:

2 ½ teaspoons yeast

2 tablespoons flaxseed meal

1 teaspoon sugar

1 cup brown rice flour

1 cup white rice flour

1 ½ cups tapioca starch

2 teaspoons xanthan gum

1 ½ teaspoons salt

3 tablespoons olive oil

Directions

Mix yeast, sugar and meal into warm water. Keep aside until it's cloudy. Whisk starch, gum, salt and rice flours in large bowl. Blend liquid into dry mixture to form dough. Add olive oil. Grease two pizza pans and place dough in them, while your hands are coated with oil. Press dough and shape to fit in pans. Keep aside for 1½ minutes to rise. Preheat oven to 425 degrees F and par bake pizza pan for 15mins. Add desired toppings and bake again for more 7 minutes till cheese starts melting.

Enjoy!

Black Bean and Chile Posole

Preparation time: 10 minutes
Cooking time: 15 minutes
Servings: 5

Ingredients

2 (4-5 inches) dried Pasilla Chilies

2 medium, leeks, cut into 2 inches chunks

2 tablespoons olive oil

4 garlic cloves, minced

2 teaspoons ground cumin

1 teaspoon dried oregano

2 (15 oz.) cans of White Hominy, rinsed and drained

2 (15 oz.) cans of black beans, rinsed and drained

1 (15 oz.) can of tomatoes, fire-roasted

Garnishes (optional)

4 cups plain tortilla chips

2 small avocados, diced

2 tomatoes, diced

4 green onions, chopped

2 limes, sliced like wedges

½ cup cilantro, minced

Hot sauce

Directions

Soften pasilla chilies. Once the seeds are discarded, puree it with the soaking liquid. Pass through a sieve and then pour the rest of the soaking liquid to it. Cut leek chunks into thin matchstick kind slices. Sauté the leeks until they are soft. To this, add the black beans, hominy, juicy tomatoes, and chili liquid with 6 cups of water. Cover the pan and boil. Once it starts to boil, simmer for 20 minutes. Arrange garnishes over the dish and serve hot.

Enjoy!

Spicy Tofu Stew

Preparation time: 10 minutes
Cooking time: 10 minutes
Servings: 5

Ingredients

1 (16 oz.) jar red peppers, roasted

2 tablespoons chili-garlic sauce or sambal oelek chili paste (Huy Fong)

2 cups vegetable broth, low sodium

1(16 oz.) package tofu, cut into 1" cubes

2 medium bell peppers, thinly sliced

1 (10-oz) package baby spinach

Directions

Mix chili paste and roasted peppers in food processor or blender until a smooth texture is achieved. Put in the soup pot with broth. Add 2 cups of water and boil. Add bell peppers, tofu cubes and simmer for 15 minutes or until the peppers feel tender. Mix spinach to it and reduce heat for five minutes. Make sure that the bright green color of spinach is maintained. Use salt and pepper for seasoning as per taste.

Enjoy!

White Mountain Mix

Preparation time: 10 minutes
Cooking time: 20 minutes
Servings: 5

Ingredients

1 cup apple rings, dried , cut into bite-size pieces

1 cup pecan halves

3/4 cup cranberries, dried

¾ cup pumpkin seeds

½ cup white chocolate chunks,

Directions

There is no cooking time for the mix. For the preparation, it is essential that all the above written ingredients are mixed together. Put them all in a large bowl and mix well. Finally, make sure that the mix is stored in a re-sealable bag.

Enjoy!

Oven-Fried Truffle "Chips"

Preparation time: 10 minutes
Cooking time: 15 minutes
Servings: 5

Ingredients

3 lbs. russet potatoes or Idaho, peeled

2 tablespoons olive oil

½ cup fresh parsley, chopped

¼ cup Parmesan cheese, grated (optional)

1 teaspoon truffle oil

Directions

Cut the potatoes in to English style' chips-½ inch thick sticks. Immerse them in a large dish with salted water, covering them completely. Bring the water to a boil for 2 minutes and drain and cool. In an oven (preheated to 425 degree Fahrenheit) arrange parchment paper and baking paper. In a large bowl, toss the potatoes and oil. Spread this in a single layer on the baking sheet of the oven and shuffle in top and bottom racks each for 10 minutes. Season with salt, pepper and toss with parmesan, parsley and truffle oil.

Enjoy!

Mushroom Wonton Soup

Preparation time: 5 minutes
Cooking time: 15 minutes
Servings: 5

Ingredients

1 12 oz. package of mushrooms, sliced

6 medium sized carrots, 1 minced, 5 sliced thinly

½ head bok choy, thinly sliced-2, rest minced

6 tablespoons fresh chives, chopped

1 tablespoon black bean sauce prepared

2 teaspoons sesame oil

4 cups mushroom broth, prepared

2 teaspoons soy sauce, low sodium

24 wanton wrappers (Twin Dragon Brand)

Directions

Put aside 1 cup mushroom sliced and mince the remaining. Mix it with minced bok choy and add the chives, minced carrot, oil and black bean sauce to make 1and half cup mix. In the mushroom broth, add 2 cups of water, soy sauce; boil. Add sliced mushrooms, carrots and bok choy; reduce temperature and simmer. Put wantons (wrappers with the mix) and add to the broth.

Enjoy!

Crispy Tofu Fingers
Preparation time: 5 minutes
Cooking time: 25 minutes
Servings: 3

Ingredients

2 to16 oz. tofu, extra firm; drained

1/2 cup cornstarch

½ cup of Flaxseed meal (optional)

1 cup rice milk or soymilk(unsweetened)

2 cups panko breadcrumbs

1/2 cup flour

1/2 teaspoon paprika

½ teaspoon of dried sage

¼ teaspoon of garlic powder

¼ teaspoon of dried ginger

¼ teaspoon of onion powder

¼ teaspoon of black pepper(ground)

Directions

Squeeze out extra moisture from tofu and cut in 16 fingers. Stir soymilk in flaxseed and cornstarch and put aside. Combine other ingredients and panko in another bowl. Immerse tofu fingers in the mixture of soymilk and later in panko mix. Ensure all sides are coated and bake in preheated oven for about 30 minutes. Make sure they are deep golden brown in color when served.

Enjoy!

Fresh Corn and Tomatillo Salsa
Preparation time: 5 minutes
Cooking time: 25 minutes
Servings: 3

Ingredients

1 ½ cups Fresh Tomatillos, husked and cut

1½ cups Corn kernels fresh

6 tablespoons Cilantro, chopped

1 tablespoon Jalapeno chili, seeded

1 tablespoon Lime juice fresh

Directions

Put tomatillos in a bowl and microwave on high power for 2 minutes. In order to cool very quickly, put in a freezer. Leave it there for 10 minutes. In a nonstick skillet heated over medium high heat, put corn, stir for a couple of minutes. Put in a larger plate and put in the freezer to cool quickly. This will take 10 minutes too. In a bowl, mix cilantro, lime juice and cilantro. Mix the corn and tomatillo sauce too, temper with seasonings like salt and pepper and serve.

Enjoy!

Mushroom Sliders

Preparation time: 5 minutes
Cooking time: 25 minutes
Servings: 3

Ingredients

Sturdy homemade buns-as per requirement

½ cup Olive oil

3 tablespoons Red wine vinegar

1 tablespoon Dijon mustard

1 tablespoon Italian seasoning

1 teaspoon Worcestershire sauce (vegetarian)

2 cloves of Garlic, chopped finely

24 large Baby bella mushrooms, stemmed

6 Deli slices of Gouda cheese, cut in quarters

24 Tomatoes, sliced thinly

24 Lettuce leaves, torn slider-size

Directions

Mix garlic, oil, mustard, Worcestershire sauce, Italian seasoning and vinegar in a bowl. Toss mushrooms in it to coat well. Marinate for 1 minute . In a preheated oven, bake mushrooms till the moisture is evaporated. To assemble, split a bun in half, arrange mushroom and

Gouda cheese and toast. Put tomato and lettuce and cover with other half of bun and serve.

Enjoy!

Jackfruit Gyros

Preparation time: 5 minutes
Cooking time: 25 minutes
Servings: 3

Ingredients

1 tablespoon Vegan margarine

1 large Onion, sliced thinly

1 20 oz. can Young jackfruit in brine, rinsed, drained and in shreds

¾ cup Vegetable broth

4 tablespoons Lemon juice

2 teaspoons Dried oregano

1 teaspoon Soy sauce, low sodium

¾ teaspoon Coriander, ground

Directions

Take a skillet and heat margarine till it starts to sizzle. Add onion and sauté till it softens (3-4 minutes). Add jackfruit and cook for 20 minutes. It should either get caramelized or get brown in color. Mix broth, oregano, half the lemon juice, coriander and soy sauce. Use seasoning like salt and pepper as per taste. Simmer till the liquid can no longer be seen or for 10-15 minutes. Put in the remaining lemon juice.

Enjoy!

Grilled Vegetable Wrap

Preparation time: 5 minutes
Cooking time: 25 minutes
Servings: 3

Ingredients

12 thin Asparagus spears, trimmed

1 red Bell pepper, ½ " strips size cut

1 Zucchini or summer squash, cut into rounds

1 clove of Garlic, chopped finely

½ teaspoon Red chili sauce (sriracha)

1 tablespoon Olive oil

½ cup White bean

2 (8-inch) Tortillas whole grain

6 Basil leaves

8 Red onion, thinly sliced

1 cup Baby arugula leaves

Directions

In a preheated broiler or grill, mix together bell pepper, asparagus, oil and squash. Put seasonings as per taste. Mash together chili sauce, garlic and beans in a bowl till smooth. To assemble, put bean mixture in tortilla, top with basil leaves, roasted veggies, onion slices and arugula. Roll tightly, chill and serve.

Enjoy!

Spicy Banh Mi

Preparation time: 5 minutes
Cooking time: 25 minutes
Servings: 3

Ingredients

¼ cup of rice vinegar (can substitute with apple cider vinegar)

2 teaspoon of agave nectar, honey or sugar

½ -1 teaspoon of flakes of red pepper

¼ cup of daikon radish, shredded

¼ cup of carrot, shredded

½ -1 baguette (French or Vietnamese), lengthwise split into half

1 tablespoon of mayonnaise, low-fat

1 teaspoon of chili sauce (red)

1 teaspoon of tamari or soy sauce (low sodium)

½ cup of baked tofu (Asian flavored), thinly sliced, or fried into tofu cubes

2-6 inch strips of cucumber

6 cilantro sprigs

6 cherry tomatoes, sliced thinly

4 lettuce leaves

Directions

Add vinegar, flakes of red pepper and honey in a bowl. Add carrot and radish to the mixture to prepare a topping. Mix well and leave for 15-30 minutes. Stir them continuously until it's combined. Now the oven should be preheated to about 350 degrees F. bake the baguette in oven till its crisp for 3-5 minutes. Let it cool down. Spread the mayonnaise on both sides of bread. Sprinkle the tamari and the red chili over it. Fill in the bread with cucumber, cilantro and tofu. Now the radish and carrot sauce should be drained onto the vegetables and spread it on them evenly. Garnish with lettuce and tomatoes and add salt and pepper to taste. Finally before serving press the baguette (top-half) on the sandwich.

Enjoy!

Kung Pao Sliders

Preparation time: 5 minutes
Cooking time: 25 minutes
Servings: 3

Ingredients

Sliders

1 14-oz. pkg. of tofu (extra-firm), patted dry

4 tablespoons of soy sauce, low sodium

2 tablespoons. of cane sugar (natural)

2 teaspoons of sesame oil, toasted

1 teaspoon of cornstarch

16 wheat buns

Slaw

3 tablespoons of soy sauce (low sodium)

2 tablespoons of vegan mayonnaise

2 tablespoons of peanut butter (creamy and natural)

5 teaspoons of cane sugar, natural

2 tablespoons of rice vinegar

2 teaspoons of sesame oil, toasted

1 teaspoon clove of minced garlic

⅛ teaspoon of black pepper, ground

1 pinch of cayenne pepper

4 8-oz of julienned carrots

2 8-oz of julienned zucchini

¼ cup of finely chopped peanuts (dry and roasted)

Directions

At first, to prepare the sliders the tofu should be sliced lengthwise, then halve the slices to increase the number. Whisk together the soy sauce, oil, sugar and cornstarch in a small bowl. Pour on the tofu until completely covered and let it cool down for about 1 minute .

Now for the slaw whisk together the soy sauce, peanut butter, mayonnaise, vinegar, sugar, garlic, oil, cayenne and pepper, in a separate bowl. Slowly stir in the zucchini, carrots and peanuts. Leave it for cooling. The oven should be preheated to 375°F. The Baking sheet should be coated with the cooking spray. Drain in the tofu, and transfer to the already prepared coated baking sheet. Bake for 25 minutes. Flip the whole tofu and bake for 20-25 minutes more until crispy. Before serving, fill in the buns with sliced tofu and 2 tablespoons of slaw.

Enjoy!

Tasty Tofu Patties

Preparation time: 5 minutes
Cooking time: 25 minutes
Servings: 3

Ingredients

¼ cup of vegan mayonnaise

¼ cup of onion, finely chopped

¼ cup of chopped parsley

2 teaspoon of dried tarragon

1 teaspoon of Dijon mustard

1 14-oz. pkg. of firm tofu

1 4-oz. can of rinsed and finely chopped mushrooms (sliced and drained)

⅓ cup of carrots, grated

4 finely chopped tomatoes (sun-dried in oil) drained

1 cup of breadcrumbs

1 16-oz. jar of tomato sauce, already prepared

Directions

Whisk together the onion, parsley, mayonnaise, mustard and tarragon in a small bowl. Prepare a mixture by mashing tofu with fork. Stir in carrots, tomatoes and mushrooms. Fold in the breadcrumbs. Heat a large sized skillet after coating with cooking spray. Scoop in the tofu mixture onto the warm skillet in 1/4th -cup of dollops. Cook for about 5 to 7 minutes until the patties are brownish golden. Flip the patties, and repeat the process. Cook as many patties required following the procedure and before serving top each patty with ¼ cup of tomato sauce. Serve in a plate.

Enjoy!

Coconut Lentils

Preparation time: 5 minutes
Cooking time: 20 minutes
Servings: 3

Ingredients

¼ cup of coconut flakes, unsweetened

1 tablespoon of coconut oil

1 ½ cups of chopped yellow onion

½ teaspoon of ground ginger

½ teaspoon of ground turmeric

¼ teaspoon of ground allspice

2 tablespoons. of tomato paste

1 cup of green lentils (French)

¼ cup of raisins

2 teaspoons of lime juice

Directions

The oven should be preheated to 350°F. Arrange the coconut flakes on a baking sheet and toast them for around 4 to 6 minutes until golden. Set them aside. Heat the coconut oil in a large sized skillet. Add the chopped onions, and sauté to about 5-7 minutes till the onions are tender. Stir in turmeric, ginger and allspice for 30 seconds till its fragrance is prominent. Stir in and sauté tomato paste, again for another 30 seconds. Add 1 cup of water to the pan, and scrape out any brown colored bits if present. Add raisins, lentils and 2 cups of water. Boil them and leave for 30 minutes in a covered vessel. Now again cook for another 10-15 minutes unless the lentils soften. Add the lime juice and finally sprinkle pepper and salt to enhance the taste. Garnish each of the serving with 2 teaspoons of toasted coconut.

Enjoy!

Portobello Cheeseburgers

Preparation time: 5 minutes
Cooking time: 5 minutes
Servings: 3

Ingredients

2 tablespoons of Bragg Aminos (Liquid)

2 tablespoons of red wine

4 oil-packed tomatoes, (sun-dried and drained) 1 tablespoon of oil reserved

1 teaspoon of Dijon mustard

⅛ teaspoon of ground black pepper (fresh)

8 Portobello mushrooms, large (stems and gills removed)

1 medium sized onion

4 oz. of goat cheese (garlic-herb)

Directions

Whisk together the 1 tablespoon of oil with the tomatoes, wine, mustard, liquid aminos, pepper and 1/2 cup of water in a bowl. Pour over the mushrooms, and let it marinate for around 10 minutes. Heat up a grill pan. Initially grill the bottom side of the mushrooms for 4 minutes; then the onion rings for 5 minutes. On a platter, transfer the mushrooms with the bottom side pointing up where each mushroom should be filled in with 1 onion ring, 1 oz. of cheese and 1 tomato. Repeat the process for all other mushrooms left. Grill burgers for 10 minutes more, until cooked thoroughly.

Enjoy!

Yellow Split Pea Dal

Preparation time: 5 minutes
Cooking time: 15 minutes
Servings: 3

Ingredients

2 tablespoons of coconut oil

1 cup of finely chopped yellow onion

2 tablespoons of 6 cloves of minced garlic

½ cup of carrots, finely chopped

1 tsp. of cumin seeds

1 tsp. of turmeric powder

2 teaspoons of flakes of red pepper

1½ cups of yellow split peas (dried)

2 tablespoons of lemon juice

½ cup of cilantro leaves (optional)

Directions

Preheat a rice cooker for 2-3 minutes. Pour in coconut oil and heat for 1 more minute. Add garlic onion, and carrots, and cook for 5-6 minutes till the vegetables become tender. Add flakes of red pepper, turmeric and cumin and cook for 1 minute more. Adjust the rice cooker settings so that the cooking process occurs slowly. Now, pour into the cooker the split peas and continuously keep on adding 4 cups of water by stirring. Add pepper and salt if desired. Finally, cover the pressure cooker and let it cook for 3-4 minute s. If desired, the dal can be thinned by adding water. Before serving add lemon juice after garnishing with cilantro.

Enjoy!

Arugula and Peach Salad

Preparation time: 5 minutes
Cooking time: 25 minutes
Servings: 3

Ingredients

10 cups of arugula

4 sliced and pitted peaches

2 cups of finely chopped green bell peppers

⅔ cup of slivered almonds

2 tablespoons of olive oil

2 tablespoons of white balsamic vinegar

1 tablespoon of orange juice (fresh)

½ teaspoons of orange zest, grated

¼ teaspoons of salt

⅛ teaspoons of cayenne pepper

Directions

Combine together the peaches, bell pepper, arugula and almonds in a large sized bowl. Separately, whisk together the olive oil, freshly prepared orange juice, the grated orange zest, the balsamic vinegar, cayenne pepper and salt, in another bowl. Before serving, the salad should be tossed properly along with the dressing.

Enjoy!

Cabbage Calzones

Preparation time: 5 minutes
Cooking time: 10 minutes
Servings: 3

Ingredients

¾ cup of 4 oz. of red potatoes (each made into ½-inch pieces)

2 cups of ¼ head of sliced and cored green cabbage

1 Tbs. of olive oil

1 cup of finely diced small onion

4 teaspoons of minced clove garlic

1 ½ tsp. of dried oregano

1 15-oz.can of chopped tomatoes

8 pitted and coarsely chopped Kalamata olives

2 teaspoons of red wine vinegar

3 Tbs. of fresh and chopped parsley

1 16-oz. package of pizza dough (already prepared)

Directions

Boil a large sized pot of saline water. Add the potatoes, and cook until they soften. Now, add the cabbage to the pot and cook until tender. Drain the water and keep it aside. Warm oil in a skillet. Into the skillet now add onion, and cook for 5 minutes until softens. Next, add oregano and garlic, and cook for 1 minute. Add tomatoes, and keep on cooking till the mixture has mostly dried up. Add vinegar and olives, and cook for 3 more minutes. Now, gently add the parsley, cabbage and potatoes into the mixture, keep stirring. Add pepper and salt to enhance the taste. Keep it for cooling. The oven should be preheated to 425°F. Use the cooking spray to coat the baking sheet. Cut the dough into 8 pieces, and roll each piece into an 8-inch of diameter circle. Now place the 1/2 cup of filling on the below half of each diameter of the circle, leaving around 3/4-inch of border surrounding the edges. Fold the dough containing the filling, and pinch the ends together so that it gets sealed. Repeat the process with the remaining pieces. Make 3 tiny slits at the top of each calzone. The calzones just prepared should be transferred to the greased baking sheet. Bake until the calzones turn golden brown. Serve.

Enjoy!

Hawaiian Pizza

Preparation time: 5 minutes
Cooking time: 15 minutes
Servings: 3

Ingredients

1¼ cups of pizza sauce

1 par-baked pizza crust (Gluten-free)

1½ cups of shredded mozzarella

½ cup of fresh pineapple, diced

1 gluten-free veggie-burger patty (crumbled and cooked)

2 teaspoons of flakes of red pepper

Directions

The oven should be preheated to 425°F. Spread the pizza sauce on the par-baked crust. Top with diced pineapple, shredded mozzarella, veggie-burger patty (crumbled), and flakes of red pepper. Bake for 5-7 minutes till the cheese melts and the toppings turn golden brown. Before serving, garnish with arugula.

Enjoy!

Grilled Salad Pizza
Preparation time: 5 minutes
Cooking time: 5 minutes
Servings: 3

Ingredients

2 tablespoons of balsamic vinegar

2 teaspoons of honey

1 teaspoon of Dijon mustard

½ teaspoons of small clove of minced garlic

3 tablespoons of olive oil

1 Chewy Pizza Dough

3 tablespoons of Parmesan cheese, grated

1 cup of arugula

1 cup of romaine lettuce, sliced

1 cup of head of red endive, sliced and halved

½ cup of fresh fennel, thinly sliced

¼ cup of red onion, thinly sliced

Directions

At first to prepare the vinaigrette: Whisk together the honey, garlic, vinegar and mustard. Coat with oil, and add pepper and salt to taste. Set it aside for 30 minutes. Next for the pizza, prepare the chewy pizza dough, and drizzle grated Parmesan. The oven should be preheated to 350°F. Then bake the pizza for about 25 minutes till the bottom is brown and crispy. Brush with 3 tabespoons of Vinaigrette at the bottom of the pizza. Now, with the rest of the vinaigrette, toss lettuce, fennel, arugula, onions and endive. Use the arugula mixture as the topping for the pizza. Finally, till the vegetables starts wilting, broil them for around 2-3 minutes. Garnish with the Parmesan curls and serve immediately.

Enjoy!

Edamame Pâté Sandwiches

Preparation time: 5 minutes
Cooking time: 15 minutes
Servings: 3

Ingredients

1 ¼ cups of shelled edamame, frozen and thawed

½ cup of walnuts

⅓ cup of packed mint leaves

1 chopped green onion

½ teaspoon of salt

3 tablespoon of lemon juice

8 slices of bread (whole-grain)

2 cups of arugula

4 jarred red peppers, roasted and drained

2 small thinly sliced cucumbers

Directions

Process the walnuts, green onions, thick edamame and the mint leaves after adding into it a pinch of salt to enhance the taste. The process should be continued until the ingredients are finely chopped. Now add the lemon juice and 3 tablespoons of water to the processor while it is running. Now, smoothen them thoroughly. Spread 1/3 cup of pâté over both the sides of each of the 4 bread slices. Finally, add 1/2 cup of arugula, cucumbers and 1 roasted pepper to each. Combine all the 8 slices and the sandwich will be ready to serve.

Enjoy!

Oven Fried Truffle chips
Preparation time: 5 minutes
Cooking time: 10 minutes
Servings: 3

Ingredients

3 lbs. of peeled russet potatoes or Idaho

2 tablespoons of olive oil

½ cup of fresh parsley, chopped

¼ cup of Parmesan cheese, grated

1 teaspoon of truffle oil

Directions

Slice the potatoes into British style chips. You will get them if you cut the chips into sticks having thickness of 0.5 inches. Transfer the chips to a large saucepan which is already filled with salted water. After boiling the water for around 2 minutes, drain it and cool the pan.

Set the temperature to 425 degree Fahrenheit for preheating the oven. After that, use the parchment paper for lining 2 baking sheets. Take oil in a big bowl and toss potatoes in it. Spread them in a line on the baking sheets and then bake them for half an minute . You have to stir the potatoes and change the baking sheets from one rack to another frequently. Then put the potatoes in a bowl for tossing them with truffle oil, parmesan and parsley.

Enjoy!

Broccoli Raab with Spicy Peanut-Miso Dressing

Preparation time: 5 minutes
Cooking time: 10 minutes
Servings: 3

Ingredients:

1 lb. Broccoli rab with trimmed ends

3 tablespoons Natural peanut butter (chunky style)

1 tablespoon Rice vinegar

2 teaspoons Miso (sweet white)

2 teaspoons Honey

½ teaspoon Chile-garlic sauce

Directions

Boil about 2 inches of water in a large pan. Add broccoli and cover the pan. Cook for about 4 minutes. Flip once using tongs and cook for 4 more minutes, till the raab is tender and vibrant green. Drain water and let it cool. Cut stem into halves. Whisk 2 tablespoons water, peanut butter, honey, miso, chili-garlic sauce and vinegar together in a bowl. Pour gently over broccoli raab and toss for even distribution.

Enjoy!

Miso-Roasted Eggplant Soup

Preparation time: 5 minutes
Cooking time: 20 minutes
Servings: 3

Ingredients:

¼ cupMiso (sweet white)

¼ cup Orange juice

1 tablespoon Mirin

2 teaspoons Brown sugar

1 tablespoon Almond oil

2 medium Eggplants sliced into ¼inch size

1½ cups Onion

½ cup Almond milk

2 tablespoons Toasted almonds

Directions

Use cooking spray to spray on foils lining 2 baking sheets. Preheat oven at 400 degrees F. Stir miso, brown sugar, orange juice, almond oil and mirin together in a bowl. Brush both surface of eggplants with the mixture. Arrange on baking sheet and top with slices of onions. Roast for 20 minutes till caramelized slightly. Transfer the whole preparation in a blender and combine with 2½ cups water and almond milk and pulse to smooth puree. Add more water for desired thickness. Sprinkle toasted sliced almonds.

Enjoy!

Three-Herb Cherry Tomato Pizza

Preparation time: 5 minutes
Cooking time: 20 minutes
Servings: 3

Ingredients:

1 ¼ cups Marinara sauce

1 Gluten-Free Pizza Crust par baked

8 oz. Mozzarella, fresh

1 ½ cups Cherry tomatoes, halved and sliced

¼ cup Parsley, fresh and chopped

¼ cup Basil, fresh and chopped

¼ cup Chives, chopped

Directions

Preheat oven at 425 degrees F. Spread marinara sauce gently over pizza crust. Use fresh mozzarella and tomatoes as toppings. Bake for around 7 minutes till cheese begins bubbling. Remove from oven and place fresh basil, fresh parsley and chives as further toppings. Serve hot.

Enjoy!

Spicy Cashew Cheese

Preparation time: 5 minutes
Cooking time: 15 minutes
Servings: 3

Ingredients

1 cup of raw cashews

3 tablespoons of lime juice

2 tablespoons of dehydrated onion, minced

2 teaspoons of lime zest, grated

¾ teaspoons of kosher salt

½ teaspoons of chipotle powder

½ teaspoons of ground coriander

½ teaspoons of ground cumin

½ teaspoons of garlic powder

Directions

Keep the cashews in a big bowl and cover it with four cups of boiling water. Use a clean towel for covering it and then soak it for the next six minute s. Drain the water and rinse the cashews. Mix the cashews with the other ingredients along with 1 tablespoons of cold water using a food processor or blender for around 5 minutes. Chill the smooth paste for 3 minutes and you are ready to serve.

Enjoy!

Grilled Serrano Salsa Verde
Preparation time: 5 minutes
Cooking time: 15 minutes
Servings: 3

Ingredients

1 bunch of fresh cilantro

¾ cups of olive oil

1 roasted or grilled serrano chili

1 tablespoon of champagne vinegar

1 large or 2 small garlic cloves in grilled form

Directions

Use a bowl present in a food processor for mixing all the ingredients along with ¼ cup water. Just mix it until it becomes a smooth paste.

Enjoy!

Berry-Apricot Salsa

Preparation time: 5 minutes
Cooking time: 15 minutes
Servings: 3

Ingredients

1 cup of divided raspberries

2 tablespoons of apricot preserves

1 cup of fresh apricots, peaches or nectarines, in diced form

1 cup of blackberries

3 tablespoons of candied ginger, chopped

Directions

Squash four raspberries in a medium sized bowl and stir in the apricot preserves for making sauce base. Mix the remaining raspberries, ginger, blackberries and fresh apricots. Keeping the berries intact, toss it carefully. You can even season it with pepper and salt if you want to. The flavors should be allowed to meld by letting the salsa stand for around 7-10 minutes.

Enjoy!

Chapter 6: Snacks and Desserts

Almond Butter Fudge

Preparation Time: 15 minutes
Cooking time: 2 minutes
Servings: 8

Ingredients:

2 ½ tablespoons coconut oil

2 ½ tablespoons honey

½ cup almond butter

Directions:

Combine coconut oil and almond butter in a saucepan and warm for 2 minutes or until melted.

Add honey and stir. Pour the mixture into candy container and store in the fridge until set. Serve and enjoy!

White Chocolate Fat Bomb

Preparation Time: 5 minutes
Cooking time: 2 minutes
Servings: 8

Ingredients:

4 tablespoons butter

4 tablespoons coconut oil

4 tablespoons erythritol, powdered

4-ounces cocoa butter

¼ teaspoon salt

¼ teaspoon Stevia

½ teaspoon vanilla extract

½ cup walnuts, chopped

Directions:

Add your cocoa butter and coconut oil into a pan over medium heat for 2 minutes or until melted, then remove from heat.

Add Stevia, vanilla extract, erythritol, salt, and walnuts. Mix well to combine.

Pour mixture into silicone mold and place in the fridge for an minute .

Serve and enjoy!

Brownie Balls
Preparation Time: 20 minutes
Cooking time: 2 minutes
Servings: 12

Ingredients:

6 dates, pitted

¼ cup chocolate chips

½ cup almond meal

2 tablespoons coconut butter

2 teaspoons vanilla extract

Directions:

Add your dates to your food processor and pulse for 3 minutes. Add all remaining ingredients except chocolate chips.

Pulse until well combined. Add chocolate chips and pulse for 2 times.

Form dough into 12 balls and place into the fridge for 1 minute .

Serve and enjoy!

Peanut Butter Fudge

Preparation Time: 15 minutes
Cooking time: 2 minutes
Servings: 20

Ingredients:

12-ounces peanut butter, smooth

4 tablespoons maple syrup

4 tablespoons coconut cream

3 tablespoons coconut oil

Pinch of salt

Directions:

Line baking tray with parchment paper. Melt the coconut and maple syrup in a pan over low heat for about 2 minutes or until melted.

Add peanut butter, coconut cream, and salt into the pan, stir well. Pour fudge mixture into the prepared baking dish and place in the fridge for an minute .

Cut into pieces serve and enjoy!

Instant Blueberry Ice Cream

Preparation Time: 15 minutes
Cooking time: 0 minutes
Servings: 2

Ingredients:

1 cup blueberries

1 teaspoon lemon juice, fresh

1 tablespoon Splenda

½ cup heavy cream

Directions:

Add all ingredients into a blender and blend until smooth. Serve immediately and enjoy!

Chia Raspberry Pudding

Preparation Time: 10 minutes

Cooking time: 0 minutes

Servings: 2

Ingredients:

4 tablespoons chia seeds

½ cup raspberries

1 cup coconut milk

Directions:

Add the raspberry and coconut milk into your blender and blend until smooth. Pour the mixture into a mason jar. Add chia seeds and stir. Cap jar and shake. Place in the fridge for 3 minutes then serve and enjoy!

Choco Mug Brownie

Preparation Time: 5 minutes
Cooking time: 10 seconds

Servings: 1

Ingredients:

½ teaspoon baking powder

¼ cup almond milk

1 scoop chocolate protein powder

1 tablespoon cocoa powder

Directions:

In a safe microwave, mug blend the protein powder, cocoa, and baking powder.

Add milk in mug and stir. Place the mug in the microwave for 3o seconds. Enjoy!

Pistachio Ice Cream

Preparation Time: 20 minutes
Cooking time: 0 minutes
Servings: 3

Ingredients:

2 egg yolks, organic

1 ¾ cups coconut milk

1 tablespoon oil

1 tablespoon honey

5 tablespoons pistachio nuts, chopped

1 teaspoon vanilla

Directions:

In a bowl, add honey, egg yolks, oil, coconut milk, salt, and whisk.

Place the mixture into the fridge for an minute . In a pan over medium heat roast chopped pistachio nuts.

Run ice cream mixture in ice cream maker and add in the roasted pistachios halfway through.

Serve chilled and enjoy!

Sparkling Lemonade

Preparation time: 10 minutes
Cooking time: 15 minutes
Servings: 5

Ingredients

1 cup sugar

A pinch of salt

2 cups fresh lemon juice

¼ teaspoon champagne yeast

Directions

Boil 1 cup water in a small saucepan. Remove from heat and mix salt and sugar in it, till completely dissolved. Cool and add lemon juice and stir again. Pour the liquid using funnel into 2 liter soda bottle. Fill bottle with water leaving a 1 inch headspace. Add desired amount of sugar. Put yeast into mixture. Screw cap and shake well for even distribution of yeast. Keep bottle on room temperature for 5-7 days, checking lemonade periodically. Refrigerate the carbonated lemonade for 2 weeks. Open slowly and gradually to avoid bubbling-up. Store it in refrigerator for better results.

Enjoy!

Sage Julep

Preparation time: 10 minutes
Cooking time: 15 minutes
Servings: 5

Ingredients:

½ cup sage leaves, torn in halves, 6 whole for garnishing

5 lemons: 3 quartered, 2 for garnishing

6 tablespoons brown sugar

12 oz. unsweetened iced tea or bourbon

¾ cup seltzer water

Directions

Freeze 6 empty tumblers. Take shaker and put 10 halved sage leaves, 1 tablespoons brown sugar and 2 lemon quarters for preparing each beverage individually. Mash together using the back of a spoon for 30 seconds, until aromatic. Add 4 ice cubes and top with bourbon or 2 oz. iced tea and 1oz. seltzer. Fill crushed ice in chilled tumblers and strain julep mixture over it from the shaker. At last garnish with sage leaf and lemon slice.

Enjoy!

Strawberry Ricotta
Preparation Time: 10 minutes

Cooking time: 10 minutes
Servings: 2

Ingredients:

2 teaspoon Splenda

1 cup strawberries, washed, sliced

½ cup ricotta cheese

Directions:

Add ricotta cheese to a shallow serving dish. Sprinkle with Splenda. Mash strawberries and pour over ricotta. Serve and enjoy!

No-Bake Raspberry Cheesecake Truffles

Preparation Time: 5 minutes

Cooking time: 10 minutes
Servings: 48 (truffles)

Ingredients:

½ cup erythritol, powdered

8-ounces cream cheese softened

1 teaspoon vanilla Stevia

Pinch of salt

1 ½ cups sugar-free chocolate chips, melted

¼ cup coconut oil, melted

Few drops of natural red food coloring

3 teaspoons raspberry extract

2 tablespoons heavy cream

Directions:

In a stand mixer blend erythritol and cream cheese until smooth.

Add the Stevia, cream, raspberry extract, salt, natural red food coloring and mix well. Slowly add in the coconut oil and continue to blend on high until it is incorporated.

Scrape down the sides of the bowl to make sure it is all mixed well. Place in fridge for 1 minute .

On a parchment-lined baking sheet scoop out the batter using a 1 ¼ inch mini cookie scoop. Should make 48 balls.

Freeze for 1 minute before coating with melted chocolate. Drop one cheesecake truffle into chocolate at a time and place back on the lined baking pan.

Place in fridge for 1 minute .

Serve and enjoy!

The Keto Lovers "Magical" Grain Free Granola

Preparation Time: 5 minutes

Cooking time: 10 minutes
Serving: 10

Ingredients

½ a cup of raw sunflower seeds

½ a cup of raw hemp hearts

½ a cup of flaxseeds

¼ cup of chia seeds

2 tablespoon of Psyllium Husk powder

1 tablespoon of cinnamon

Stevia

½ a teaspoon of baking powder

½ a teaspoon of salt

1 cup of water

Directions:

Preheat your oven to 300 degrees Fahrenheit

Line up a baking sheet with parchment paper

Take your food processor and grind all the seeds

Add the dry ingredients and mix well

Stir in water until fully incorporated

Allow the mixture to sit for a while until it thickens up

Spread the mixture evenly on top of your baking sheet (giving a thickness of about ¼ inch)

Bake for 45 minutes

Break apart the granola and keep baking for another 30 minutes until the pieces are crunchy

Remove and allow them to cool

Enjoy!

Pumpkin Butter Nut Cup
Servings: 5

Preparation Time: 15 minutes
Cooking time: 0 minute

For Filing

½ a cup of organic pumpkin puree

1/2a cup of almond butter

4 tablespoon of organic coconut oil

¼ teaspoon of organic ground nutmeg

¼ teaspoon of organic ground ginger

1 teaspoon of organic ground cinnamon

1/8 teaspoon of organic ground clove

2 teaspoon of organic vanilla extract

For Topping

1 cup of organic raw cacao powder

1 cup of organic coconut oil

Directions

Take a medium-sized bowl and add all of the listed ingredients under pumpkin filling

Mix well until you have a creamy mixture

Take another bowl and add the topping mixture and mix well

Take a muffin cup and fill it up with 1/3 of the chocolate topping mix

Chill for 15 minutes

Add 1/3 of the pumpkin mix and layer out on top

Chill for 2 minutes

Repeat until all the mixture has been used up

Enjoy!

Unique Gingerbread Muffins

Servings: 12

Preparation Time: 15 minutes
Cooking time: 10 minutes

Ingredients

1 tablespoon of ground flaxseed

6 tablespoon of coconut milk

1 tablespoon of apple cider vinegar

½ a cup of peanut butter

2 tablespoon of gingerbread spice blend

1 teaspoon of baking powder

1 teaspoon of vanilla extract

2-3 tablespoon of Swerve

Directions:

Preheat your oven to a temperature of 350 degrees
Fahrenheit

Take a bowl and add flaxseeds, sweetener, salt, vanilla, spices and coconut milk

Keep it on the side for a while

Add peanut butter, baking powder and keep mixing until combined well

Stir in peanut butter and baking powder

Mix well

Spoon the mixture into muffin liners

Bake for 30 minutes

Allow them to cool and enjoy!

The Vegan Pumpkin Spicy Fat Bombs

Servings: 12

Preparation Time: 10 minutes
Cooking time: 10 minutes

Ingredients

¾ cup of pumpkin puree

¼ cup of hemp seeds

½ a cup of coconut oil

2 teaspoon of pumpkin pie spice

1 teaspoon of vanilla extract

Liquid Stevia

Directions:

Take a blender and add all of the ingredients

Blend them well and portion the mixture out into silicon molds

Allow them to chill and enjoy!

The Low Carb "Matcha" Bombs

Servings: 12

Preparation Time: 10 minutes
Cooking time: 20 minutes

Ingredients

¾ cup of hemp sees

½ a cup of coconut oil

2 tablespoon of coconut butter

1 teaspoon of matcha powder

2 tablespoon of vanilla extract

½ a teaspoon of mint extract

Liquid Stevia

Directions:

Take your blender and add hemp seeds, matcha, coconut oil, mint extract and Stevia

Blend well and divide the mixture into silicon molds

Melt the coconut butter and drizzle them on top of your cups

Allow the cups to chill and serve!

The No-Bake Keto Cheese Cake

Servings: 4

Preparation Time: 20 minutes
Cooking time: 0 minutes

Ingredients

For Crust

2 tablespoon of ground flaxseed

2 tablespoon of desiccated coconut

1 teaspoon of cinnamon

For Filling

4 ounce of vegan cream cheese

1 cup of soaked cashews

½ a cup of frozen blueberries

2 tablespoon of coconut oil

1 tablespoon of lemon juice

1 teaspoon of vanilla extract

Liquid Stevia

Directions:

Take a container and mix all of the crust ingredients

Mix them well and flatten them at the bottom to prepare the crust

Take a blender and mix all of the filling ingredients and blend until smooth

Distribute the filling on top of your crust and chill it in your freezer for about 2 minutes

Enjoy!

Raspberry Chocolate Cups

Servings: 12

Preparation Time: 20 minutes
Cooking time: 10 minutes

Ingredients

½ a cup of cacao butter

½ a cup of coconut manna

4 tablespoon of powdered coconut milk

3 tablespoon of granulated sugar substitute

1 teaspoon of vanilla extract

¼ cup of dried and crushed frozen raspberries

Directions:

Melt cacao butter and add coconut manna

Stir in vanilla extract

Take another dish and add coconut powder and sugar substitute

Stir the coconut mix into the cacao butter, 1 tablespoon at a time, making sure to keep mixing after each addition

Add the crushed dried raspberries

Mix well and portion it out into muffin tins

Chill for 60 minutes and enjoy!

Exuberant Pumpkin Fudge

Servings: 25

Preparation Time: 10 minutes
Cooking time: 20 minutes

Ingredients

1 and a ¾ cup of coconut butter

1 cup of pumpkin puree

1 teaspoon of ground cinnamon

¼ teaspoon of ground nutmeg

1 tablespoon of coconut oil

Directions:

Take an 8x8 inch square baking pan and line it with aluminum foil to start with

Take a spoon of the coconut butter and add into a heated pan; let the butter melt over low heat

Toss in the spices and pumpkin and keep stirring it until a grainy texture has formed

Pour in the coconut oil and keep stirring it vigorously in order to make sure that everything is combined nicely

Scoop up the mixture into the previously prepared baking pan and distribute evenly

Place a piece of wax paper over the top of the mixture and press on the upper side to make evenly straighten up the topside

Remove the wax paper and throw it away

Place the mixture in your fridge and let it cool for about 1-2 minutes

Take it out and cut it into slices, then eat

Conclusion

The eBook has been written for those people who are not only health conscious, but also for those people who want to prepare exciting vegetarian dishes. Veggies are not only full of roughage and fibers, but also help in maintaining a complete balanced diet. The ingredients in the eBook are written perfectly with the tips and their actual quantity. The best thing about the eBook is that I have made sure that I have used the most cheaply available products in the market. Each and every ingredient can be gathered from the market, and I have also shown my different experiment with texture and taste. In the eBook we also find that vegetarian dishes not only include the main courses, but also deserts and sweets. The dishes give you a fine dining experience and even make you have a healthy diet control.

The path to a healthy body and mind is paved with fresh, wholesome, and real food. Everyone knows that eating more vegetables and grains are good for them. However, for beginners, this can be difficult because easy to make, and prep recipes are hand to find. This cookbook offers more than 100 approachable and delicious meatless recipes.

Go into this with a full force and reap all the benefits that come with it. Your mind will be in the zone and you will enjoy a healthier lifestyle. Keep in mind that you are not saying "no" to anything, but simply finding ways to enjoy the things that you love without the things that are detrimental to your health.

Wishing you a happy and healthy vegetarian lifestyle!

MACRO DIET RECIPES

BY LAUREN MCLAUGHLIN

with Sidney Kennedy

BLUEBERRY
PROTEIN PANCAKE

Recipe Makes: 1 serving

INGREDIENTS

1 SCOOP PROTEIN
½ CUP OATS
½ CUP LIQUID EGG WHITES
½ SHREDDED ZUCCHINI
¼ CUP BLUEBERRIES
STEVIA TO TASTE

FOOD PREP FOCUS

Heat a non-stick pan over low heat. In a small bowl, gently mix protein powder, egg whites, oats, zucchini and stevia together. When combined, fold in fresh blueberries. Spray pan with coconut oil cooking spray and add a generous scoop of pancake mix. Cover and cook over low heat until bubbles rise and pop through cake (about 4-5 miutesn). Gently flip pancake and cook additional 2-4 minutes until cooked thoroughly.

MACROS

41 PROTEIN
42 CARB
4 FAT
8 FIBER

360 calories

SWAPBOX

Swap blueberries for 1/4 cup shredded apple or 1/4 cup organic pumpkin puree.

VEGGIE FRITTATA

Recipe Makes: 2 servings

INGREDIENTS

1 CUP EGG WHITES
1 WHOLE EGG
1 CUP GREEN VEGGIE
1/4 CUP YELLOW OR WHITE ONION
1/2 CUP MUSHROOMS
1/4 CUP LOW FAT MILK OR ALTERNATIVE
1 CLOVE GARLIC
1/4 CUP LOW-FAT OR DAIRY-FREE MOZZARELLA
CHOPPED BASIL/CILANTRO FOR GARNISH
SALT AND PEPPER TO TASTE

FOOD PREP FOCUS

*Pre-heat oven to 375 degrees. Chop onion and garlic. Par-cook
mushrooms and green veggie of your choice (spinach, asparagus,
etc.). Spray quiche dish or oven-safe skillet with non-stick spray.
Whisk eggs, milk, salt and pepper togther. Add egg mixture and veggies
to dish. Place in pre-heated oven and cook for 35-40 minutes.
Cool and serve.*

MACROS

31 PROTEIN
27 CARB
6   FAT
8   FIBER

282 Cals

SWAPBOX

Swap cheese and replace with 1/4 fresh avocado.

BLACK BEAN SOUP

Recipe Makes: 4 servings

1 ONION, CHOPPED
1 CELERY RIB, CHOPPED
1 TBSP CRUSHED GARLIC
1 TSP THYME
1 (14.5 OZ) CAN BLACK BEANS, DRAINED
8 CUPS VEGETABLE BROTH
1 TSP GROUND CUMIN
1 (14.5 OZ) CAN DRAINED BLACK BEANS
½ TSP DRIED SAGE
1 TBSP OLIVE OIL

Heat oil in large stock pot over medium heat. Cook onions, celery, garlic and thyme until soft, about 7 to 10 minutes. Add black beans, 4 cups vegetable broth and the cumin to the pot. Mix and combine. Stir in beans. Add remaining vegetable broth and sage. Bring to a gentle boil and simmer 30 minutes. Cool and serve.

12 PROTEIN
42 CARB
4 FAT
12 FIBER

260 Cals

ASIAN
LETTUCE WRAPS

Recipe Makes: 4 servings

INGREDIENTS

1 LB GROUND TURKEY (99% LEAN)
1 CUP SLICED MUSHROOMS
½ CUP THINLY SLICED SCALIONS
4 TBSP POWDERED PEANUT BUTTER
1 TBSP SESAME OIL
1 TBSP RICE VINEGAR
8 OZ CAN WATER CHESTNUTS (DRAINED AND CHOPPED)
3 CLOVES MINCED GARLIC
2 TBSP FRESH GINGER (GRATED/MINCED)
1 HEAD LETTUCE (WASHED / SEPARATED)

FOOD PREP FOCUS

Cook turkey on stovetop until no longer pink. Drain off excess liquid. Add mushrooms and cook for 4-5 minutes. Add remaining ingredients (except lettuce) and continue cooking a few more minutes. Spoon mixture into lettuce, wrap and serve!

MACROS

30 PROTEIN
8 CARB
6 FAT
2 FIBER
196 Calories

SWAPBOX

With 93% lean turkey: 246 calories, 25 Protein, 8 Carb, 12 Fat

TURKEY LASAGNA

SERVINGS

Recipe Makes: 4 servings

INGREDIENTS

8 OZ EXTRA LEAN GROUND TURKEY
1 BOX BROWN RICE PASTA NOODLES
2-3 ZUCCHINI (THINLY SLICED WITH PEELER,
MANDOLIN OR SPIRAL CUTTER)
2 CUPS WHITE SAUCE (BLEND 1 CUP WALNUTS, 2-4
CLOVES GARLIC, ½ TSP SEA SALT, 1 CUP WATER, AND
JUICE FROM ½ LEMON)
1 ½ PRE BAKED SWEET POTATOES
1 LARGE ONION, CHOPPED AND CARAMELIZED
1 TSP OREGANO
1 TSP BASIL
½ TBSP OLIVE OIL
SEA SALT TO TASTE

FOOD PREP FOCUS

Preheat oven to 350. Cook turkey on stovetop. Caramelize onions in olive oil and pinch of salt. Spray lasagna dish with non-stick cooking spray. Mash cooked sweet potato with caramelized onions with oregano and basil. Layer: ½ inch layer of mash mixture to bottom of dish; uncooked noodles; white sauce; turkey; zucchini; sprinkle of salt; white sauce. Cover and bake for 1 hour. Remove cover and cook another 15 min. Cool slightly and garnish with fresh chopped basil.

MACROS

13 PROTEIN
46 CARB
12 FAT
5 FIBER

338 calories

GRILLED SHRIMP WITH
SALSA FRESCA

SERVINGS

Recipe Makes: 1 serving

INGREDIENTS

6 OZ SHRIMP (PEELED, GRILLED OR PAN SEARED)
1/2 CUP FRESH TOMATOS
1/4 RED ONION (RED OR WHITE)
1/2 GREEN BELL PEPPER
1/4 JALAPENO
1/2 AVOCADO
FRESH LIME JUICE
FRESH CHOPPED CILANTRO

FOOD PREP FOCUS

Chop salsa ingredients on cutting board.

Gently combine and top with shrimp.

MACROS

40 PROTEIN
23 CARB
14 FAT
10 FIBER

369 Cals

SWAPBOX

Swap shrimp for chicken breast or omit avocado for lower fat recipe.

EASY
CHICKEN PHO

Recipe Makes: 1 serving

4 OZ. GRILLED CHICKEN BREAST
1/2 CUP RICE NOODLES
1/2 CUP LOW SODIUM CHICKEN BROTH
1/2 CUP JULIENNED CARROTS
SLICED CUCUMBERS
SLICED JALAPENOS (OPTIONAL, TO TASTE)

Cook rice noodles according to package directions. Heat chicken broth over medium heat and add carrots, cooking gently. Add grilled chicken, rice noodles and remaining ingredients.

27 PROTEIN
36 CARB
4 FAT
5 FIBER

280 Cals

GREEN BEAN SALAD

Recipe Makes: 4 servings

INGREDIENTS

1 POUND GREEN BEANS (ENDS TRIMMED)
1 POUND GRAPE TOMATOES (HALVED)
3 TBSP OLIVE OIL
2 TSP BALSAMIC VINEGAR
3 TBSP RAW SUNFLOWER SEEDS
2 TBSP FRESH THYME
JUICE OF ½ LEMON
SALT AND PEPPER TO TASTE

FOOD PREP FOCUS

Trim ends off green beans. Boil water and cook green beans al dente.
Cut tomatoes and herbs. Blanch green beans and cut if desired
Gently toss all ingredient. Can be served warm or cool.

MACROS

5 PROTEIN
18 CARB
14 FAT
5 FIBER

204 Cals

SWAPBOX

Swap sunflower seeds for sliced almonds or toasted pine nuts. Add lean
protein for complete meal. For lower fat meal, omit oil and nuts.

COD &
KALE SALAD

Recipe Makes: 1 serving

INGREDIENTS

4 OZ COD FISH (BAKED)
2 BUNCHES KALE, SLICED TO THIN STRIPS
1 GREEN APPLE, SLICED
2 TSP SHELLED PISTACIOS
1/4 CUP SLICED DRIED FIGS

DRESSING:
1 TBSP OLIVE OIL
JUICE OF 1/2 LEMON
JUICE OF 1/2 ORANGE
SALT AND PEPPER

FOOD PREP FOCUS

Bake white fish as normal in oven. Toss kale, apple, nuts, figs into a bowl. Whisk dressing ingrediesnts and toss with salad.
Top with baked fish.

MACROS

30 PROTEIN
39 CARB
2   FAT
7   FIBER
504 Cals

QUINOA SALAD

Recipe Makes: 4 servings

INGREDIENTS

1 CUP QUINOA
2 CUPS WATER
1 BUNCH SCALIONS
1 BUNCH PARSLEY
1 BUNCH FRESH MINT
1-2 LARGE TOMATOES
1 TBSP OLIVE OIL
JUICE OF 2 LEMONS
1 TBSP BRAGG'S LIQUID AMINOS
SALT, PEPPER AND CHILI POWDER TO TASTE

FOOD PREP FOCUS

Rinse dry quinoa rubbing the grains together to remove hull. Place water and quinoa in a saucepan. Bring to boil. Reduce heat to a simmer and cover. Cook for 10 to 15 minutes or until all water has been absorbed.

While quinoa is cooking, mix together the chopped tomato, chopped parsley and scallions. Add lemon juice, olive oil, aminos and fresh mint to tomato mixture. Stir in cooked quinoa and seasonings. Mix well and chill in refrigerator until eating.

MACROS

8 PROTEIN
37 CARB
6 FAT
5 FIBER

222 calories

SALMON WITH
MISO GLAZE

Recipe Makes: 2 servings

INGREDIENTS

2 (6 OZ) SKINLESS SALMON FILLETS
1/8 CUP WHITE MISO PASTE
1/8 CUP MAPLE SYRUP
1/8 CUP COCONUT AMINOS
1 TBSP GINGER
1 TBSP SESAME OIL/OLIVE OIL
1 CUP SUGAR SNAP PEAS

FOOD PREP FOCUS

In a large bowl, whisk together the miso, maple syrup, aminos, ginger and sesame oil. Add salmon and toss to coat. Preheat the broiler and adjust rack to about 6 inches from the heat. Line a baking sheet with parchment and place the fillets on the sheet. Broil until the glaze is browned and shiny and the salmon is firm and opaque, about 5-8 minutes. In the meantime, steam the snap peas and cook until crisp-tender, about 5 minutes.

MACROS

33 PROTEIN
22 CARB
9 FAT
3 FIBER

294 calories

SHRIMP FAJITAS OVER
BROWN RICE

Recipe Makes: 1 serving

INGREDIENTS

4 OZ SHRIMP (PEELED)
BELL PEPPER (ANY COLOR), CUT INTO THIN STRIPS
½ ONION SLICED INTO HALF RINGS
SALT-FREE FAJITA SEASONING BLEND
¼ CUP BROWN RICE

MACROS

27 PROTEIN
25 CARB
2 FAT
5 FIBER

226 calories

TACO BOWL

SERVINGS

Recipe Makes: 1 serving

INGREDIENTS

5 OZ LEAN GROUND TURKEY
¼ CUP BLACK BEANS OR KIDNEY BEANS (RINSED)
FRESH SALSA OR PICO DE GALLO
ANY OTHER FRESH VEGGIES
½ MED-LARGE AVOCADO
SALAD GREENS OF CHOICE
2 TSP CHIA SEEDS
1 TBSP HEMP SEEDS

MACROS

38 PROTEIN
18 CARB
13 FAT
9 FIBER

346 calories

RICE CAKES WITH
TUNA SALAD

SERVINGS

Recipe Makes: 1 serving

INGREDIENTS

1 CAN OF LOW SODIUM TUNA
CHOPPED CELERY, RED ONION, CUCUMBER AND
PARSLEY
1 TBSP LOW-FAT MAYONNAISE OR VEGANAISE
1 TBSP DIJON MUSTARD
LETTUCE LEAVES
3 BROWN RICE CAKES

MACROS

38 PROTEIN
50 CARB
12 FAT
5 FIBER

452 calories

TURKEY
AVOCADO WRAP

Recipe Makes: 1 serving

INGREDIENTS

5 OZ 99% LEAN GROUND TURKEY
1/4 CUP PINTO BEANS, DRAINED AND RINSED
2 TBSP FRESH SALSA
CHOPPED LETTUCE, UNLIMITED AMOUNT
1/2 AVOCADO
1 LARGE SPROUTED GRAIN TORTILLA

MACROS

43 PROTEIN
42 CARB
17 FAT
14 FIBER

495 calories

SWAPBOX

Swap pinto beans for black beans. For gluten-free option, swap sprouted grain tortilla with brown rice tortilla.

TURKEY CHILI

SERVINGS

Recipe Makes: 4 servings

INGREDIENTS

16 OZ 99% LEAN GROUND TURKEY
1 CONTAINER OF SALSA
1 CAN OF BLACK BEANS (RINSED AND DRAINED)
1 CAN OF KIDNEY BEANS
1 RED ONION, CHOPPED
1 RED BELL PEPPER, CHOPPED
1/2 JALAPEÑO, DICED (OPTIONAL)
HANDFUL OF FRESH CILANTRO
3 ROMA TOMATOES, DICED
1 TSP CHILI POWDER
SEA SALT AND PEPPER TO TASTE

FOOD PREP FOCUS

Add raw turkey to a crock pot first, breaking up with a wooden spoon. Season with 1 tsp pink sea salt. Add everything else and cook slow on low for 6 hours. You may also cook on stove top for 5 to 6 hours.

MACROS

31 PROTEIN
38 CARB
9 FAT
11 FIBER

400 Cals

BAKED FISH &
BRUSSELS SPROUTS

Recipe Makes: 1 serving

INGREDIENTS

7 OZ WHITE FISH (BAKED)
½ CUP BROWN RICE
15-20 BRUSSELS SPROUTS (TRIMMED AND HALVED)
1 TBSP OLIVE OIL OR COCONUT OIL
2 TBSP MINCED GARLIC
JUICE OF 1 SMALL LEMON
1 TBSP BRAGG'S LIQUID AMINOS
½ CUP CHOPPED ONION (OPTIONAL)
SRIRACHA (OPTIONAL)

FOOD PREP FOCUS

Preheat oven to 400 degrees. Cook fish separately as desired. Mix remaining ingredients together in a large bowl, being sure to coat the Brussels well. Cover a baking sheet with foil or Silpat. Spread the mix on the baking sheet, making sure the brussels are spread out in a even layer. Sprinkle with sea salt and fresh ground pepper. Cook Brussels until tender. Set oven to broil and cook brussels another 5–10 minutes until the edges get golden brown.

MACROS

40 PROTEIN
45 CARB
9 FAT
11 FIBER

415 calories

YOGURT PARFAIT

Recipe Makes: 1 serving

INGREDIENTS

1 CUP FAT-FREE GREEK YOGURT
1/2 CUP FRESH FRUIT
STEVIA DROPS TO SWEETEN

FOOD PREP FOCUS

Mix stevia with yogurt and top with fruit of your choice.

MACROS

19 PROTEIN
18 CARB
0 FAT
2 FIBER

143 Cals

SWAPBOX

Swap fruit with cacao nibs, pomegranate seeds or other fruit.

COCONUT FRO-YO

Recipe Makes: 1 serving

1 SCOOP VANILLA PROTEIN POWDER
1 SCOOP GLUTAMINE POWDER
1 CUP UNSWEETENED COCONUT MILK
STEVIA TO TASTE
2 HANDFULS ICE

Blend ingredients in high powered blender.
Serve and enjoy!

21 PROTEIN
6 CARB
6 FAT
1 FIBER

147 Cals

Printed in Great Britain
by Amazon